# *The*
# LAWS OF GREAT ENLIGHTENMENT
## *Always Walk with Buddha*

IRH Press

*The*
# LAWS OF GREAT ENLIGHTENMENT
*Always Walk with Buddha*

# RYUHO OKAWA

IRH Press

**BOOKS**
IRH PRESS
New York

ISBN 13: 978-1-942125-62-4
ISBN 10: 1942125623

Printed in Turkey

First Edition

# CONTENTS

CHAPTER ONE

# THE ENEMY IS WITHIN YOU

## *Do Not Let Your Mind Control You But Control Your Mind*

# 3 Attaining a State Free from Desire

# 4 Being Liberated Through Wisdom

CHAPTER TWO

# The Power to Forgive Sins

*Have the Courage to Forgive
Both Yourself and Others*

## 1 Try to Live a Better Life, Rather than the Perfect One

## 2 Bearing the Suffering Caused by a Crime or Accident

## 3 Begin Afresh with a Strategy of Withdrawal

# 4 The Courage to Forgive Yourself

# 5 The Courage to Forgive Others

# 6 Mistakes Are Also Valuable Experiences

# 7 Try to Achieve a Turnaround Within Your Lifetime

# 8 Believe in a World that Transcends the Rational

# CHAPTER THREE

# WORK ABILITY
# AND ENLIGHTENMENT

### *How to Become a Person
Who Can Bring Happiness to Many*

## 1 Shakyamuni Buddha Was Highly Competent at Work As Well

## 2 Enlightenment in Zen Buddhism—Shen-hsiu and Hui-neng

# 3 Problems with Zen that Teaches Sudden Enlightenment

# 4 Work Ability and Enlightenment Are Interrelated

CHAPTER FOUR

# THE MOMENT OF GREAT ENLIGHTENMENT

*The Mystical Multi-Dimensional Space
Revealed by the Great Enlightenment*

# 3  The True Nature of Energy

# 4  The Mission of Religion

CHAPTER FIVE

# ALWAYS WALK WITH BUDDHA

### Study the Laws of the Mind and
### Put Them into Practice All Through Your Life

## 1  What Is Your True Self?

## 2  What You Come to See Through Meditation

## 3  The Freedom of the Mind

## 4 Peace of Mind

## 5 Missionary Work Means Spreading Wisdom

## 6 The Law of Cause and Effect

## 7 Strive to Master the Laws of the Mind

# PREFACE

This book is the seventh in my "Laws" series. I put all my thoughts and energy into the completion of this book. Readers who have continued to read my books will probably find its contents profound and meaningful. Even beginners will be able to feel the enthusiastic engagement of my writing as they read this book, because it fully expounds on the main themes of enlightenment and forgiveness.

I have imbued this book with the strong will of "seeking enlightenment above and saving people below," which is the fundamental theme of Buddhism. Please read and savor it again and again, until you find yourself shedding tears. Although the themes presented in this book may be difficult, I have explained them in a most easily understandable and contemporary way that a true religious leader should do. What's more, my teachings give abundantly clear answers to the various questions of life.

The Buddhist term, "Great Enlightenment" (Daigo), essentially means clearing away all delusions and becoming one with absolute Truth. But in this book, I use it to mean it the attainment of a deep and great enlightenment (Taigo) that anyone can experience, for I want to share its gentle yet profound feeling with you who are reading this.

*Ryuho Okawa*
*Founder and CEO of Happy Science Group*
*December 2002*

Chapter One

# The Enemy Is Within You

### *Do Not Let Your Mind Control You*
### *But Control Your Mind*

# 1
# Becoming Liberated Through Faith

## Angulimala
## —How did this young man become a murderer?

This chapter is on the theme, "The enemy is within you." It will mainly serve to guide you to become the master of your mind. Let us begin with a story from India, which took place in the time of Shakyamuni Buddha.

One of the two main locations where Shakyamuni Buddha gave his teachings was the Jetavana Monastery, located in Shravasti, the capital of the kingdom of Kosala. Shravasti has long since become ruins. These days, apart from the few people who make their living from the sightseeing business, no one lives there, which reminds me of the Buddhist saying, "All things are transient."

The Jetavana site is now a lush green park somewhere between 5.7 and 6.5 acres in size—though some say it is as big as 16 acres. In the brick remains of Jetavana, the platform where the Buddha gave his sermons still exists even to this day. The site is now called Saheth.

Less than a mile from Saheth is the Buddhist site Maheth, where a stupa, the religious memorial to a man named Angulimala can be found. The stupa is much larger than you would expect; the moment you see it, you may find it odd and out of place and wonder, "Why is there such a large stupa for Angulimala in a place like this?"

Many events took place in Jetavana involving Buddha's disciples, and the story of Angulimala is a famous one. Angulimala was a native of Shravasti, and was held in high regard by later generations of the local people.

What kind of man was Angulimala? The name is often translated as a "wearer of a garland of fingers," but his original name according to many sources was Ahimsaka or, to quote another source, Ahimsa. Given that Ahimsaka means "harmless" or "no harm" (it can also be translated as "incompetent"), it may have also been a label or nickname given to him after his death.

Ahimsaka was a disciple of a notable Brahmin, someone of the priestly class in the Hindu caste system. While living in the Brahmin's home at Shravasti, he learned the ascetic disciplines. He was a bright, handsome young man and showed great promise as a student of Brahmanism.

One day when the Brahmin was out, his wife attempted to seduce Ahimsaka. However, he resisted the temptation, saying, "I am still in training, and my teacher's wife is equal to a mother for me. I could never imagine having that sort of relationship with you."

The rejected middle-aged woman could not accept such injury to her pride, so she sought revenge in a very underhanded way. When her husband returned, she cried, "Ahimsaka tried to rape me," after having ripped her own underwear and skirt.

The Brahmin became outraged. But he thought to himself, "As a respected teacher I cannot use brute force and beat my disciple physically." (Another source says he thought he would lose in a physical fight with the young man.) So he decided to ruin the young man's life with a treacherous plot.

When he met Ahimsaka, he told him, "You are doing very well in your ascetic training. Now, I will give you one last challenge to master. If you are able to accomplish it, you will attain enlightenment, be granted all the secrets of the Truth and be qualified to have its full mastery. Try to complete it."

The Brahmin handed him a sword and commanded him, "Go into the village every day and kill people. Take one thousand lives in total, cut a finger off each person and make a necklace out of their fingers."

Many sources say that it was "a thousand" so I have adopted this version, but according to other sources, it was a hundred. It would have been quite hard for one man to actually kill a thousand people, so this statement may well be the type of exaggeration often used in Indian lore. Of course even if it was one hundred, it is still a large number of people. I assume that Angulimala actually did kill a great number of people, for he was notorious as for being a vicious murderer.

The residents of Shravasti went into a wild panic. Every night, a demon-like man would appear and murder people. After killing them, Ahimsaka would cut a finger off each one, and then link the finger to a necklace. Because he wore this necklace when he went out to murder, he was called Angulimala, "he who wears a garland of fingers." Legend has it that, after having killed nine hundred and ninety-nine people and with just one last killing to reach his goal, Angulimala was about to kill his own mother as his last victim.

## The Buddha's strong admonition

Shakyamuni Buddha decided to save the young man who had strayed from the right path by admonishing and leading him to repentance. The people of Shravasti would shake with fear every night at the appearance of the demoniacal murderer. So the Buddha went out of the Jetavana Monastery to seek Angulimala in order to exorcise this living devil.

Angulimala was found frantically trying to kill his own mother, Mantani. But when he saw the Buddha coming near, he decided to change the target of his attack and focused on the Buddha, his sword above his head. However, no matter how hard he tried, he was unable to get close the Buddha; through his supernatural power, the Buddha had moved away from him, as if gliding.

Unable to understand what was happening, Anguli-mala cried out to the Buddha, "Stop!" The Buddha turned to him and replied, "I am standing still. It is you who are moving." (According to another source, he said, "I have stopped. Angulimala, you should also stop.")

On hearing the Buddha's words, which were like a Zen koan or riddle, Angulimala, in total confusion, said to himself, "I went after him but I could not reach him. That is impossible unless he was moving. Yet, he says he is standing still and it is I who is moving. Is that possible?" He was completely bewildered.

Angulimala was thus given a Zen-like riddle to open his eyes. This episode illustrates why the Zen sect originated out of mainstream Buddhism.

What did the Buddha mean by these words? Of course, in physical terms the Buddha was actually walking. In fact, he meant, "My mind is completely still. It is your mind that is wavering."

The Buddha's intended message was, "My mind is calm. My inner world is as quiet as still water or the tranquil surface of a lake, without a single ripple. On the other hand, your mind is wild and rough like angry waves. You are in a frenzy without any ability to discern good from evil, and all you are thinking of is your final victim to achieve your goal of one thousand. Whoever you see, whether it is your mother or anyone else, your eyes will become fiery and you will burn with anger like an Ashura demon. My mind is completely still. It is actually your mind that is moving and agitated." This was actually an analogy to show Angulimala the malevolence of his mind while the mind of the Buddha was at peace.

Angulimala was struck by the divine power of the Buddha's words which opened his eyes; it was the power of the Dharma. Trembling, he fell to the ground in amazement, thinking, "I have never experienced anything like this before."

Buddhist scriptures often exaggerate in the style of myths, and they describe this scene in the following way: "At that moment, all his hair suddenly fell out and he became as bald as a monk, while his garments turned into Buddhist robes." No one in the present day would take this description literally, but I assume it symbolizes the change that took place in Angulimala's mind when he suddenly realized his wrongs and became a monk.

"Oh, please forgive me. Make me your disciple," said Angulimala falling to the ground in full prostration and pledging devotion to the Buddha. As a result of the Buddha's strong admonition, the man who had killed nine hundred and ninety-nine people (or ninety-nine according to other sources), and was hunting for his last victim, shed tears in repentance of his past crimes and begged to be allowed to join Shakyamuni Buddha's order.

"Good. Follow me," the Buddha said and accepted Angulimala as his disciple.

## Angulimala undergoes spiritual discipline
## While stones are thrown at him

Upon hearing that Angulimala had joined the priesthood, the people of Shravasti became excited with disbelief. They shouted, "The new order of Shakyamuni Buddha is popular and attracts the faith of many people but look, they have taken in that terrible murderer Angulimala as a disciple!"

By that time, King Prasenajit of Kosala had arrived with his army to capture Angulimala. He had come in response to the pleas of the people, who had told him of the dreadful evildoer and asked him to capture the murderer by any means possible to restore peace to the area. On the way to capture the outlaw, the king encountered the Buddha and his disciples.

The Buddha asked, "King, what is the matter?"

"I have come to capture a terrible evildoer named Angulimala."

"Angulimala is here, following me."

When the King saw Angulimala with his shaven head, wearing the robes of a monk, he thought, "No matter how terrible he has been, he is now a disciple of the Buddha, so I will not attempt to detain him. Instead, I must give him alms." So he returned to his palace without capturing him.

The people of Shravasti, however, could not forgive Angulimala because many of them had lost loved ones in the killings. Many stood up to condemn him.

"We will never forgive that man. How inexcusable of Shakyamuni Buddha's order to accept him as a disciple!"

Whenever Angulimala went into the village to beg for alms, people threw rocks at him, and he would return bleeding. "When I go out for alms I cannot get anything. People stone me instead," Angulimala cried out to the Buddha.

The Buddha taught him, "You are now undergoing valuable spiritual discipline to dissolve your past sins. Endure it." Hearing this, Angulimala continued his spiritual training, enduring his bloody wounds. Then eventually, people started to accept him.

## Angulimala saves a woman
## Having a difficult delivery

One day when Angulimala was going out to ask for alms, he came upon a woman who was having difficulty in giving birth. (Another source says that on seeing Angulimala, the woman became so terrified that it caused her to have a troublesome delivery.) Angulimala quickly returned and reported this to the Buddha, "A woman is suffering a difficult delivery, unable to give birth to a child. What can I do for her?" The Buddha answered, "I will give you a *gatha*. Go back to the woman and chant it, then her baby will be born safely."

Gatha is a Sanskrit word meaning a short verse or song that expresses the heart of the Dharma. The Buddha chanted the gatha: "Since I was born, I do not recall that I have ever deprived a living being of life. By the power of this virtue of mine, may the mother and baby be well."

To explain this gatha further, it means, "I have never killed any living thing from the time I was born, and I have the power of the Dharma that comes from my virtue. By this power, the mother and child will be blessed, allowing a safe birth."

On hearing this, Angulimala was very surprised. "I have killed nine hundred and ninety-nine people and I am so notorious that there isn't one person who hasn't heard of my deeds. So if I said that, wouldn't it be a lie? I could never say it. A pure-hearted high priest could say it, but if I, a former villain, said it, no one would believe my words. It wouldn't have any effect, would it?"

However, the Buddha replied, "Just chant it as I have told you." (Some sources say that the Buddha explained the real meaning of the words, which was that since Angulimala had awakened to become a child of the *Tathagata*, or a disciple of the Buddha, he had not killed any living thing.)

As the Buddha had directed, Angulimala returned to the woman and chanted, "Since I was born, I do not recall that I have ever deprived a living being of life. By the power of this virtue of mine, may the mother and baby here be well." In a short time, the child was born safely.

## Enlightenment has the power to purify past sins

This episode illustrates the fact that even a man like Angulimala, who had murdered so many people in the past, can be redeemed if he pledges devotion to the Buddha's teachings, changes his heart and diligently disciplines himself; all his past sins will be erased while he is still alive. The purification will extend back to the day he was born. Enlightenment has the power to effect such changes.

The point is this: Human beings accumulate various wrongdoings after they are born into this world. But if you encounter the Buddha, believe in Him, undergo spiritual training and attain a certain level of enlightenment, all past wrongdoings will be purified and disappear, as if they have been wiped away. Then you will be exactly like a pure, innocent and immaculate holy practitioner of spiritual training, who has never committed any sins.

What the Buddha teaches here is that even if someone has committed murder, by devoting himself to the teachings of Buddha and awakens to the Truth, the sins he committed in years gone by will actually be erased in this lifetime and will not be carried over into the next life.

There are in fact cases where people committed crimes and were imprisoned, but then encountered the teachings of Happy Science, causing them to awaken and later become devoted and faithful believers. The past sins of people like that can be recorded as crimes in this earthly world, but if, by encountering the Buddha, the person repents deeply and has a change of heart to become a light to the world, it would be the same as never having committed any sin from the day he or she was born.

And more, if that person then becomes able to save others by sharing his or her light, he or she will be able to generate further positivity and become an embodiment of light. Not only are the person's own sins from the past cancelled, but he or she will also be given the power to clear away the sins and impurities of many others. This is the power of Buddha's Truth, and the story of Angulimala teaches this truth.

## Liberation through faith

The story of Angulimala is a well-known Buddhist legend and has had much influence in later stories and teaching. For example, part of the story is used in the famous Japanese story of Benkei and Ushiwakamaru.* A warrior monk named Benkei confronted Ushiwakamaru,

---

* Ushiwakamaru was the childhood name of Minamoto-no-Yoshitsune, a general of the Minamoto clan in the 12th century. He was the younger brother of the first Kamakura shogun, Yoritomo. In his early teens, Ushiwakamaru met Benkei and defeated him in a dual. Benkei then decided to serve Ushiwakamaru as a loyal retainer.

as Benkei was on a personal quest to collect the swords of other swordsmen by dueling with them and was looking for his thousandth sword.

I presume that the teaching of Shinran's True Pure Land sect of Buddhism, particularly Shinran's idea that Amitabha Buddha places the salvation of evildoers above the salvation of the virtuous, was also largely influenced by the story of Angulimala. I have stated before that the teachings of the True Pure Land sect and their lineage are one extreme in Buddhism and can be considered quite heretical. But if I were to search for the origins of the True Pure Land teachings in Buddhist scriptures apart from the Three Pure Land Sutras, one source would be the story of Angulimala.

I have also stated a few times before that the teachings of the True Pure Land sect of Buddhism and the teachings of Christianity have much in common. Looking at the story of Angulimala, we can find in Buddhism certain aspects that are similar to Christianity.

After all, the story of Angulimala teaches how a person can be liberated through an act of faith. Attaining liberation through faith means "By devoting oneself to the Buddha, the Dharma, and the Sangha, one can be released from the bonds of past sins, or errors in one's thinking, and attain freedom."

In the True Pure Land stream of Buddhism, this is the equivalent of the idea that by believing in Amitabha Buddha and chanting His name, one can find salvation. In the case of Christianity, this is equivalent to the idea that if you believe in Christ, you can enter the gates of heaven. But Christian faith is different from that of Amitabha Buddha, as it teaches there is a final judgment before salvation.

Angulimala was a native of Shravasti. Looking at the large stupa that still stands in the town, we can understand just how famous he was. The sensational story of this notorious evildoer, who did a 180 degree turn to become a renowned disciple of the Buddha, must have been passed down from generation to generation with a sense of drama.

What we must learn from this story is that while the soul of human beings have particular tendencies from birth, it does not mean that everything is predetermined by destiny. It is also important to remember that although we can judge a person by looking at the way he or she has lived for the past few decades, this does not mean a person will continue to live in the same way. A completely new life can begin when an unearthly religious power works upon the soul. This power enables an entire life to change, back to its earliest beginnings.

# 2

# Be the Master of Your Own Mind

## A "precept body" to protect you
## From evil temptations

Why did Angulimala commit sins? Let us consider this point. He had been training intensely under a Brahmin; he was a good student and had a promising future. But because he was a handsome young man, his teacher's wife desired him and tried to seduce him. His rejection of her led the wife to behave resentfully. She lied to her husband, and the angry husband ordered Angulimala to kill a thousand people. Unable to disobey his teacher's command, he began to murder, and his mind became so vicious that finally, he even attempted to kill his own mother. Then he met the Buddha and everything changed; by repenting and devoting himself to the Buddha, his past was cleared away and he was able to start a completely new life.

His was indeed a stormy life and just listening to his story, it may have seemed that Angulimala's life was completely at the mercy of external elements. The

Buddhist scriptures actually relate this story as if he was not to blame at all. However, was it really true that he had no faults? On consideration, it may not necessarily be the case.

Angulimala was a handsome young man and, to some extent, he may well have had sexual desires typical of a man of his age. Those desires could have been apparent. Although he may not have acted upon them, I assume that there was something in his heart that attracted temptation.

Buddhism has many rules, among them the Five Precepts. For those who constantly observe these precepts an aura called a "precept body" forms around them, though it cannot be seen. As you observe certain precepts, you will gradually radiate this sort of aura.

For example, if someone has made the decision, "I will never kill any living thing" and keeps that vow for ten or twenty years, then a distinctive aura will emanate from that person. A teacher has a distinctive air that is specific to teachers, a monk has a monkish air, a judge has a magisterial air, and a police officer the air of a lawman. In the same way, if you undergo spiritual training while observing certain precepts, an invisible spiritual aura known as a precept body will form, and this will protect you from all kinds of temptation.

If you observe the precepts, even if a wrongdoer approaches you to try to tempt you into committing some bad act, he will be repelled like oil to water. When he comes close to you with an intention to deceive you, he will be repelled by something like an aura emanating from you. So he cannot tempt you.

Those who observe precepts have the distinctive aura of a precept body that has formed around them. So even if an evildoer might try to tempt them with the words, "I have a good money-making idea. I know where hidden treasure is, so let's go get it!" he could not actually bother them, since he would somehow sense that they are unapproachable.

Therefore, those with precept bodies will naturally avoid any possible wrongdoing. Evildoers will tend to stay away from such people because the qualities of their wavelength are so different.

The same holds true for children at school. When children fall into bad company and do something wrong, parents often complain, "There are bad kids at school; they lured my child to do this awful thing." However, they cannot necessarily say their child was completely without fault.

There is a spiritual law, "the Laws of Same Wavelengths' Attraction," and if a child has some element in his or her nature that is attuned to negativity, he or she will naturally be attracted to others with the same tendencies, eventually joining a group of delinquents. If, on the other hand, there is some element within the child that repels wrong, troublemakers will not come near him or her. They will sense, "He cannot fit in our company," or "She is not like us," and will automatically keep a distance from him or her.

According to the legend, Angulimala was diligently undertaking spiritual training and was highly intelligent and a promising student, but from a Buddhist point of view, it seems his precept body was not yet fully formed and there still was some weakness in his mind. We can assume that there was something in his subconscious that attracted negativity.

### The ability to judge good from evil
### Is unrelated to academic ability

Several years ago in Japan, a religious cult committed a serious crime that was similar to the story of Angulimala. At that time, more than ten people died and several thousand were injured. This is a much higher number than the nine hundred and ninety-nine people that Angulimala is said to have killed. Members of this cult were allegedly planning to kill even more people using poison gas and other methods. This means there was a group of disciples who, following their teacher's guidance, would have been willing to kill ten thousand people. This is a trap typical of religious cults.

The media reported that it was unbelievable that highly educated people—graduates of top-tier universities such as the University of Tokyo, Waseda or Keio University—belonged to the cult and that when they were ordered to kill, they did so without any hesitation. Circumstantially, it is very possible because there is almost no correlation of academic ability or intelligence to the emotional problems that arise in relationships between men and women or the ability to distinguish good from evil.

People make mistakes when dealing with the opposite sex regardless of whether or not they are intelligent. Some people, though they are not academically competent, still have highly developed morals and are able to discriminate between good and evil, while others who are academically able may not possess good moral sense.

There is not necessarily any correlation of a person's academic ability or educational background to one's moral or emotional behavior and sensitivities. At school there are no tests for these sorts of issues nor are there any classes that teach such knowledge.

In schools, relationship issues are barely taught. Concerning good and evil, although simple judgments about what is good and what is bad are taught in the early years of elementary school as part of moral education, it is not later taught as a proper academic subject. Therefore, the ability to distinguish between good and evil does not necessarily bear any relation to a person's academic ability; it largely depends on a person's outlook on life, as well as the environment they have experienced.

## Wisdom exists to make people happy

In the story of Angulimala, the problem lies not only with the teacher who ordered him to kill a thousand people, but also with the disciple who chose to follow a teacher like that and obey his orders without a second thought. This particular teacher-disciple relationship was the result of a lack of wisdom, or to use a Buddhist term, "ignorance."

Angulimala thought he could attain enlightenment if he practiced what his teacher told him, but the level of understanding here is the same as that of a company employee who blindly follows instructions. It is the same as saying, "My supervisor told me to do it, so I did it exactly as he said." This often happens in companies and government offices.

As long as an employee follows the orders of a supervisor, he won't have any problems. However, the company may be doing something illegal, such as disposing of dangerous substances that contaminate an area, causing many people to suffer from the pollution. If the employee knows that the substances are harmful, morally speaking, he or she should insist the activity be stopped, even if he or she is ordered to dispose of the pollutants. From a broader perspective or an ethical standpoint, that is how the employee should act.

Take for example the case of the Ministry of Health and Welfare of Japan (currently the Ministry of Health, Labor and Welfare) ignoring the danger of AIDS caused by contaminated blood products. At the time, some officials could have recognized the potential danger and taken preventive measures so that there would not be any victims.*

In the workplace, there are many cases where employees are forced into difficult situations presented by supervisors who want to save face. They may be told, for instance, "We must do this for the sake of appearances," or "Because I am in this position, business with that company will be done my way." To follow the orders of superiors and simply do as they say is quite easy, but the excuse, "I just followed instructions," is only valid for matters inside their organization.

This is what happened in the cases of Angulimala and the aforementioned Japanese cult. However, be it Brahmanism, Buddhism, or any other religion, if you are a true practitioner undertaking spiritual training on the path of Truth, you need to be aware of the foundation of the path of Truth.

In fact, Truth is based on love and compassion for many people, and wisdom exists to nurture people and make them happier. To achieve this end, the practitioners of Truth are undertaking spiritual training.

---

* In the 1980s, about 1,800 haemophilia patients in Japan contracted HIV through tainted blood products due to the continued use of non-heat-treated blood products for infusions. The Ministry of Health and Welfare at the time was accused of not taking any countermeasures to prevent more cases occurring.

This being the case, is it ever possible for someone undertaking spiritual training toward a given goal to do the exact opposite to achieve that goal? In the case of the story of Angulimala, could he really achieve enlightenment and qualify as having mastered the Truth by killing a thousand people? No, it could never be possible.

## Do not cling to titles and qualifications

Angulimala did not understand that true mastery of the Truth was in acquiring the power of enlightenment, an unseen power; instead, he was only attracted by an endorsement supposedly confirming the attainment of enlightenment.

In life, similar cases often occur. Suppose you study flower arrangement or the tea ceremony. If your aim were to master the spirit of the art and to work on it for the rest of your life, you would not be bothered by whether or not you could obtain some certificate or qualification. However, if your aim was only to achieve recognition so that you could show off your certificate to others, you would do anything to get it.

People of the latter type tend to resort to illegal methods when, for example, they want to enter a university. Using bribery they will buy their way into university or do it by some connection that is obviously beyond their position. After getting into a school, if they find passing the exams difficult, they once again maneuver or bribe professors to allow them to graduate.

People who believe that credentials have power and aim solely to obtain entrance qualifications or diplomas will act like this. They will desperately try to get qualifications at any cost, believing that only if they have them will they be able to get a good job, marry a good partner, or get quickly promoted and succeed.

On the other hand, those who really want to pursue academic studies and who genuinely enjoy studying would never act in this way. If these people were to find it difficult to pass exams and graduate, they would admit that their performance had not been adequate and put in another year of effort to get through. Even if they were unable to get a degree, after leaving university, they would continue to follow the path of study on their own. This is the right way and a sensible attitude.

However, those who believe solely in the power of qualifications do not act in this way. We can often see these kinds of people in today's society. They value, for example, their academic background or the status of their company. Even in top-flight companies there are many people who are incompetent at work, but some believe themselves to be among the highest ranking just because they are working for a leading company. When these people change jobs, they will reveal themselves to be incompetent at any kind of work. On the other hand, there are also people who believe that regardless of the company they work for, those who do top quality work are first-rate people. These types of people will be successful even if they change jobs.

Those who cling to worldly qualifications or ostentatious titles, believing that these represent their level of enlightenment, academic ability or social status, are largely mistaken. You should not lose sight of what is basically the right way.

## The cause of failure lies within oneself

It is insane to think like Angulimala, who was so eager to attain enlightenment that he would even kill a thousand people, or even worse sacrifice his own mother's life. The big mistake was in his inability to understand that the underlying thinking was crazy.

The problem lies not only with the teacher who duped him but also with Angulimala himself, who became the disciple of this kind of man, and believed that he was actually undergoing a spiritual training. His sin was "ignorance," or lack of wisdom.

Earlier I mentioned the Japanese cult which committed serious crimes. Some people pleaded on behalf of the followers saying, "It was only the leader who was insane. The followers had been brainwashed, they were victims." However, I do not agree with this.

Whether highly educated or not, those who committed murder believing they could attain enlightenment without any twinge of conscience, and those who did nothing to stop the fatal orders from being carried out had within them something similar to the darkness of the person who issued those orders. They cannot blame others for what they themselves did. They should know this.

The enemy is always within. It is not other people who cause you harm, nor is it the orders or judgments of others that bring about your failure. The cause of your failure is always to be found within yourself, in your own mind.

The mind cannot be seen with physical eyes, but it is present in everyone. You have to be very careful not to let your mind control you. Do not allow your mind to be your master; be the master of your own mind.

The mind is like an invisible living thing; it can suddenly produce various thoughts and desires to do different things. For example, some people will impulsively grab or steal an object they want the moment they see it in a department store, only to be discovered and arrested by the police. This happens because, at the very moment of the theft, they are being controlled by that invisible mind.

Similar temptations are to be found everywhere. For instance, there was a bank clerk who had been working at a bank for twenty years. She was an experienced worker so her supervisor had entrusted an entire section in her care. In that position, she was able to slightly alter the records to withdraw money from the bank without anyone noticing. She had a dissolute boyfriend, who squandered money gambling on boat and horse races, and he demanded that she give him more money if she wanted them to stay together. So she falsified the bank records and took money from the bank over and over again to give to him.

The poor woman simply thought, "I don't want to lose my boyfriend so I'll have to give him more money. Because my salary is not enough, I have no choice but to take the bank's money." Certainly, this is the tragedy of a person who has failed to master her own mind and let her mind become the master.

She was driven by her feelings and let her mind control her. She should have held on to the part of her who took control of her mind, to look at herself from a higher standpoint and ask herself, "What will happen if I do this? Am I doing the right thing?" Once again, the chief mistake lay in the fact that her mind was the master and she became a slave to it.

# 3

# Attaining a State Free from Desire

## The five human desires

Human beings have five basic desires. First, there is the desire for property and money. Since this world is based on economic principles, in modern society we cannot live a single day without spending a penny. It is impossible to live without spending any money, no matter how free of desire we may be. We cannot do anything about this. Beggars also have the desire for property because they too cannot live without some kind of financial resource.

Next comes the desire for sexual love, otherwise called lust. This is the desire for the opposite sex and this too is deeply rooted in the human mind.

There is also the desire for eating and drinking. No matter how strongly you resist, if you do not eat you will grow hungry.

Another is the desire for fame. This is the longing to have a good reputation or be a celebrity. It is natural to crave the good opinion of others, for instance having people comment, "She is clever," "He is among the elite," "From a good family," "Graduated from a good school," "He works for a leading company," "Very successful in her career," "Qualified as a lecturer when very young."

This desire for fame is also deeply rooted.

Then there is the desire for sleep. Again, you cannot resist it. You may think you are able to work without sleep, but it is actually not possible to stay awake for more than three days. Some say they could keep on working much longer, but they may only pretend to be awake when they are actually sleeping. The desire for sleep cannot be denied either.

Human beings cannot be free of these five desires. Living as human beings in this world, we cannot deny our desire for property, sexual love, food, fame, or sleep. However, committing suicide to do away with these desires is also wrong, since it goes completely against the purpose of our soul training. If you had not been born into this world, you would not be troubled by these five desires, but as long as you live in this world, you cannot escape them. (Note that in Buddhism, the "five desires" sometimes refer to the desires that arise in connection with the five senses—sight, sound, smell, taste, and touch.)

## Both poor and rich have the desire for property

Some people may feel that the desire for money comes from already having it. They believe having money leads one to seek more of it; therefore, the desire for money can be removed by denying money and wealth. However, if you become poor, will your desire for money disappear?

This is not necessarily the case.

When I traveled to India in 1996, I visited the site of the former monastic university of Nalanda, which was founded over fifteen hundred years ago and said to have been home to over ten thousand of Buddha's disciples at its peak. It was a huge complex with a dining hall, living quarters and places for spiritual training. Of course, only ruins remain today and there are no monks living there now. The only people seen there these days are the caretakers and the tourists that come and go.

The caretakers who clean and maintain the site are most likely employed by the government. Whenever Japanese tourists pass by, they repeatedly ask for ballpoint pens with outstretched arms. This is a sad situation. Where do they think they are working? It is a significant historical Buddhist site, a holy place where Buddha's disciples underwent spiritual training, but the caretakers are only thinking of ballpoint pens, and whenever they see a Japanese person, they put out their hands and ask for one. They abuse people's spirit of charitable giving.

When we left the Nalanda ruins, our car was mobbed by about thirty beggars. They completely surrounded the vehicle and kept touching it with their muddy hands until the windows became quite smeared. Even though we wanted to get out of the car, they pressed in so closely we could not do so. Their greed was so strong that it resulted in their getting nothing. Surrounded by a crowd of thirty people who would have forced their way in, we could not open the doors or the windows and there was no way that we could give them anything. The car itself became quite dirty, so we had no option but to drive away.

If they had been able to overcome their greed and form a single orderly line to receive something, the first five or so at least would have been able to receive some money, though not all of them would have gotten a donation. When the next tourist appeared, they could have taken turns to be one of the five in the front to receive something and then afterwards they could have divided what they were given amongst themselves. By dividing the alms like this, each person's share would have been bigger. But as it was, they came from all sides like a school of piranhas, causing the tourists to flee, and ended up without a single rupee.

Of course they are extremely poor and live hard lives; anyone receiving a basic wage would not behave in such a manner. They were desperate because they would not eat that day unless they were able to get something.

From this we can see that people are not free from the desire for property just because they are poor. Poor people too have the desire for property.

Many people in India do not have the benefit of an education and if they have many children they would find it harder to make ends meet. In some cases, when a child is born into beggarhood, the mother will cut off one of its arms as an act of "mercy." By doing this, she will make the child's appearance even more pitiful, thereby increasing the child's chances to survive as a beggar for the rest of his life.

A child with only one arm would be unable to work. All who saw him could tell why he was forced to beg and they would give money out of pity. So there are some parents who will purposely cut off the arm of one of their children in order to provide him with a means of getting alms for life.

People like this, who are unable to do any physical work apart from begging, need to look as wretched as possible if they are to survive. Anyone without a physical defect would find life as a beggar difficult but it would be more obvious for someone with a handicap, such as a bad foot or a bad hand, to get money. In order for a beggar to obtain money, the worse their physical appearance or the bigger the defect, the better. This is why some parents actually maim their children.

Therefore, it is not always true to say that people who make a lot of money in business have the desire for property, whereas people without money do not have it. The desire for property is strong even among the poor.

To look at this subject from the opposite point of view, let us consider the case of the extremely rich. For example, John D. Rockefeller was a very wealthy American business magnate. He was already successful when only in his twenties and by the time he was in his forties, he had become the head of a large company making vast sums of money. Eventually he created a huge business monopoly, but by the time he had reached his fifties, he was being denounced by many for causing the suffering of others through his considerably profitable businesses. While still in his fifties, he looked like a decrepit old man. He had stomach problems and insomnia, and his health suffered greatly.

Feeling remorse for all he had done, he had a total change of heart. Determined to use his financial power to help the people of the world, he established the Rockefeller Foundation. Using his great financial resources, he built many churches, hospitals, and schools. So vast was Rockefeller's financial wealth that he contributed great amounts to the world. From that time on he lived his life guided by positive thinking, which made it possible for this man, who had almost died in his fifties, to live a long life and eventually die at the age of ninety-seven.

Therefore wealthy people, too, can have the desire for property. As rich as Rockefeller was, he would conduct business with the feeling that every single penny counted. As a result, his life became miserable, and eventually he fell ill, having reached his limit. However, by finding the spirit of giving, he changed over to a completely new life.

Rockefeller the millionaire changed his thinking, from how much money he could amass for himself to how much he could give for the good of the world. This released him of his guilt, stopped the public denunciations and indignant complaints of others, and enabled him to lead a happy life afterward. This is a good example of the victory of a wealthy man over his desire for property. So, the desire for property is held by both the wealthy and the poor.

## The desire for sexual love
## And the desire for eating and drinking

As well as a desire for property, everyone has sexual desires. For both male and female, if there was no desire for the opposite sex, married life in this world would not be possible. Because of the love between the sexes and marriage, the soul training of the human race has been able to continue.

If everyone longed for just one person of the opposite sex among the billions of people in the world and never felt any affection for any other, the human race would have become extinct long ago. But in reality there are many people whom one can like, as well as people one dislikes, so that many different couples are able to be created. This has enabled the human race to continue throughout its long history.

However, one's passion for those of the opposite sex has to be well controlled; otherwise it will be the cause of unhappiness. Romantic relationships that are blessed by others will form the basis of an ideal society, while an unblessed relationship will often give rise to overly strong attachment.

Problems involving love affairs can sometimes cause people's hearts to become so demonical that one will stab another to death or even set fire to the other with gasoline. The problems of affection are deep rooted.

Here again, the question is whether or not you can become the master of your own mind. You should not allow your mind to be the master, nor be swayed by it.

Similarly, you need to moderate your desire for eating and drinking. While eating too much can affect your health, fasting for spiritual discipline will not make you a saint; you will be unable to think of anything but food. Neither of these two paths is the right way.

## The desire for fame and the desire for sleep

There is also the desire for fame. As long as you are making efforts on the right path, with the aspiration to cultivate and develop yourself, you should be glad of others' assessments of you becoming increasingly positive. However, human beings including practitioners of spiritual training, are apt to have too strong a desire for fame, so it is necessary to always view your abilities objectively.

Ask yourself, "What is the actual level of my abilities? Do I deserve this much praise at this level? Is it too much to want to be thought of more highly?" Check and see that you are not overconfident or placing too high a value on yourself.

If you run your own business and think too highly of yourself, in most cases you will fail. When you want others to evaluate your performance, capabilities or endeavors to be higher than you actually deserve, you are taking love from others, and this will cause others' opinions of you to start to fall.

If you have too strong a desire for fame, people will question why you put so much emphasis on getting promoted, and wanting a better position that you don't deserve. And when your desires for both property and fame become too strong, people will comment, "You don't work very hard, yet you want a higher position and salary? You should ask for that when you are working ten times harder than you are now."

Lastly comes the desire for sleep. It is natural for everyone to have a moderate desire for sleep but usually, for most people, eight hours sleep is sufficient. Just three hours sleep a day is not necessarily something to admire, because you would then be unproductive when you are awake. On the other hand, sleeping all day long is being lazy. Finding a balance is very difficult. Although the length of time you sleep is not the only determining factor, sleep is very important to regulate your physical condition so you are able to continue doing good work and lead a fruitful life.

## Liberation of the mind
## —Freeing yourself from desire

The five desires for property, sexual love, eating and drinking, fame, and sleep are part of being human. If we denied them altogether, we would no longer be able to survive in physical bodies, so we cannot deny these desires. We can, however, control them. It is essential to be the master of your own mind, to take command of the five desires, and not be swayed by them.

In the first section of this chapter regarding the story of Angulimala, I talked about liberation through faith. There are other kinds of liberation, for example, the liberation of the mind. Although this can be explained in many ways, briefly it is freeing yourself from all kinds of desires, including the five desires I have just discussed.

In everyday life, your mind is likely to be torn apart by the desires that arise out of human nature. Liberation of the mind means becoming free from these desires. This is already a considerable level of enlightenment and it is very difficult to achieve this state.

# 4

# Being Liberated Through Wisdom

## Liberation through wisdom
## —Using wisdom to cut off delusion

There is also liberation through wisdom. Liberation through wisdom means dissolving delusion and becoming free by acquiring knowledge of Buddha's Dharma, or the Truth. While the Dharma-gate for liberation through faith is very wide, the gate of liberation through wisdom is also essential. This approach is to acquire a correct understanding of which cause leads to which effect, and to do away with delusion and doubt.

If I were to take the case of Angulimala, he was instructed by his teacher to kill a thousand people in order to become enlightened, and he actually tried to do this. However, with the right understanding of the Truth, he should rationally have understood that killing a thousand people would never lead him to enlightenment. In actual life, though, a countless number of people act like Angulimala and simply follow the orders of their superiors just as they are told, without giving any thought to the context of the orders.

If Angulimala had wisdom, he would have thought, "It is impossible to achieve enlightenment by killing a thousand people. If enlightenment involves such an act, then I would wish to do without it." This is liberation through wisdom. He was actually deceived by the word "enlightenment," so what he had to do was to see through this deception by the use of wisdom.

## Know the law of cause and effect

With a deeper understanding of the relationships of cause and effect, on many occasions you will be able to see clearly which cause will lead to which result. For example, there was a time when people in Japan believed that the supply of real estate was limited and it would only increase in price no matter what. Buying land was believed to be the best way to utilize one's assets, giving rise to a speculative property boom throughout the country.

During the so-called "bubble economy," which lasted from the late eighties into the nineties, bankers and accountants recommended to their clients that they invest in land. They claimed that land was guaranteed to rise in value, it would be more profitable to buy real estate than to leave money in the bank. They pointed out that land was indestructible so there could be nothing more secure to invest, and that by buying land they would be able to reduce their tax bills while increasing their assets.

I myself knew for a fact that this kind of situation could not last, so Happy Science refrained from speculating on real estate at that time. But some religious groups did not realize this and invested heavily in land with the result that their assets have since decreased and they now find themselves in financial difficulties.

While it is good to make a profit by doing proper business, speculation on land will not continue to be profitable all the time. There are alternately good times and bad, so it is very difficult to gain more than you lose. Rather than expend your energy in activities like speculation, you need to be engaged in right work and this will serve as the basis for further development. This is true with any sort of business. With sufficient knowledge, you can avoid bankruptcy. If you accumulate a certain amount of knowledge, you can avoid crises, and this kind of worldly effort is also important.

After all, everything arises from the mind, which includes happiness and unhappiness. What is important is to control your mind, not to be controlled by it. Do not let your mind be the master; instead be the master of your own mind. Always be aware: The enemy is within you.

*Chapter Two*

# THE POWER TO FORGIVE SINS

*Have the Courage to Forgive
Both Yourself and Others*

# 1

# Try to Live a Better Life,
# Rather than the Perfect One

## More deaths resulting from suicide
## Than from traffic accidents

The theme of this chapter, the power to forgive sins, is a fundamental principle of religion. It is not taught in school and it is also very rare for people to properly learn it after they have become member of society. Because of the media's daily coverage of everyone's wrongdoings, people may naturally develop the "power of not forgiving sins," but I presume it is quite uncommon to be presented with the opportunity to learn the power of forgiving sins.

I decided to take up this subject as the result of a certain piece of data. In Japan, the number of deaths from traffic accidents is less than ten thousand per year, and the number has recently been decreasing [at the time of the lecture]. There is another cause of death for an even higher number of people, and that is suicide.

The recent prolonged economic stagnancy no doubt has played a role in this, but over the past few years, the annual toll has reached over thirty thousand for people who have taken their own lives; this is more than three times the number of people who die in traffic accidents.*

These figures can be further broken down to show that roughly twenty thousand men and ten thousand women commit suicide.

These are huge numbers. If we assume that one generation lasts thirty years, in the course of a generation approximately one million people take their own lives. This is about the same number of victims as from a major war. The fact that one million people die in the course of a single generation means that it is as if the country is continuously waging war.

Even in an actual war, it is rare for a single country to repeatedly suffer losses of thirty thousand every year. During the Vietnam War, the Americans did not have such a high yearly death rate, so this gives you some idea of what a large number it is. Why does this kind of situation persist?

In Japan, efforts to solve the problem of suicide are still insufficient. This indicates a lack of fundamental thinking, such as basic philosophies, religious teachings or moral principles, for clarifying the causes of suicide and taking preventive measures.

Christian countries of the West, for example, have a religious education where people learn that committing suicide is wrong. For this reason, even if a person wishes to put an end to his life, he would naturally think twice,

---

★ According to the 2018 statistics, deaths from traffic accidents were 3,532, while the number of suiciders was 20,598.

pondering that committing suicide may not lead him to heaven. Of course there will still be people who commit suicide, but to a certain extent religious education acts as a deterring force.

In Japan, however, materialistic views are rampant and many people believe that everything ends with death. Even if people believe in the other world, they presume that upon death they will be free of their current suffering. I have to point out that true religious knowledge is woefully lacking.


## After death
## What happens to those who commit suicide?

Are all those who commit suicide condemned to end up in hell? The answer is that they do not all necessarily go to hell; the majority will find themselves at the stage just before hell. While some souls will go immediately to hell, most do not even go there. Being unable to understand that they are dead, they retain their attachments to their lives on Earth and continue to live in much the same way as people who are still alive, or they become earth-bound spirits and wander around in places where they met their death.

In this way, they remain attached to the people and things of this world, and are incapable of even moving on to hell. If they did go to hell, their suffering would of course become more apparent, but many of them are unable to move on to that stage.

So, is it absolutely impossible for those who commit suicide to enter heaven? No, it is not necessarily the case. If we look at Japanese history, for instance, the 19th-century *samurai* and political leader Takamori Saigo took his own life, as did Maresuke Nogi, a General of the Japanese Imperial Army of the 20th century.* However, neither of them are now in hell. They doubtlessly suffered when they died, but afterwards they returned to the heavenly world and became gods. They did not fall to hell mainly because they had pure minds and they were admired by a great number of people while they were alive. In this way, sometimes other principles can be at work.

However, in most cases when a person commits suicide in an attempt to escape from this world, it is very rare for that person to enter heaven immediately; it hardly ever happens. It is extremely difficult to enter heaven especially for those who have had no knowledge of the Real World while alive. Even if angels come and try to explain the situation to them, they do not accept what they are told. People who did not listen to the advice of others in the world on Earth will most likely act in the same way in the other world as well.

---

* Takamori Saigo [1828 - 1877] was the leader of the Satsuma Rebellion against the newly formed Meiji government. Upon realizing the failure of the revolt, he committed *seppuku* taking his own life. Maresuke Nogi [1849 - 1912] committed suicide following the death of the Emperor Meiji.

## People who rush into death
## Share a tendency for perfectionism

I would now like to consider the reasons people commit suicide. While living in this world, human beings make efforts in various ways in their search for happiness. Numerous ideas are taught to help them achieve happiness. However, it is impossible to avoid unhappy experiences altogether. As long as there is happiness, unhappiness in the relative sense will also arise in this world, and some people commit suicide when they have an unhappy experience. Of those who commit suicide, there may well be some who die happy, but they are probably a tiny minority. The vast majority of those who commit suicide do so because they are unhappy.

So why do people choose to take their own lives? If we look at the background of this self-destruction, we see that there can be numerous causes. For instance, there are many people who kill themselves because they are suffering from an illness. They feel they cannot bear the pain any longer and choose to kill themselves. Recently there also have been an increasing number of suicides among the elderly. They do not feel physically well and think that they will be a burden to their family or feel they have nothing to live for. There is no end to the number of old people who take their lives for this reason.

There are also young people who commit suicide as a

result of problems connected to love, marriage or divorce. And as the economic environment continues to slump, there will be people who kill themselves for financial reasons. In an effort to escape from economic difficulties, they will decide to kill themselves.

There are also people who choose to kill themselves for reasons of honor, though this is only a small percentage. People with a high social status, such as politicians, sometimes choose death to protect their honor when they are involved in some kind of case or scandal.

In this way there are numerous reasons for suicide, but primarily it seems that too many people are ill-adapted to living in this world. I would like to offer some thoughts why this may be.

In general, religions often teach people how they should live as children of God or Buddha but here I would like to suggest something different. People who commit suicide share a strong tendency to expect perfection of themselves and of others around them, and it is this excessive attitude that leads so many to rush into death. These people have a low tolerance to life's "bacteria," that is to say, to disappointments and failures or the reproaches and criticism of others which they face in the course of their lives. Their resistance to these negativities is not strong enough. The fundamental reason for this is that they demand too much perfection of themselves and others.

## Human beings are imperfect creatures

If you can look at yourself objectively, you will realize that you are not perfect or without flaws. And just as you are imperfect and flawed yourself, so are those around you. It is impossible to expect perfection of oneself and of others. Despite this, there are still a countless number of people who seek a perfection that can hardly be expected but end up living imperfect lives.

No one who claims to be a perfectionist is actually living a perfect life. People who make such statements are the very ones who live in rather imperfect ways. There is a large number of people who do not live or act in the ordinary manner like ordinary people; they flee from the battles that people should naturally be engaged in, and avoid things that people should normally overcome, all the while claiming themselves to be perfectionists.

All they do is evade their responsibilities and avoid failure; they run away, not wishing to continue any kind of fight. For whatever reason—perfectionism, narcissism, self-glorification or the idolization of others—many people are too involved in the search for perfection or beauty, but end up living in a way that is not beautiful.

It is as if they proclaim that the clothes and underwear they wear every day must be brand-new. But even if clothes or underwear become soiled, once they are washed or sent to the dry cleaners they can be worn again. They may no longer be brand-new, but in normal life we consider them clean as if new and continue to wear them.

In the same manner, you should not glorify yourself too much or be bound by rigid or unnecessary demands. Do not consider your life is over just because you have failed once. This kind of thinking is utterly disrespectful of those who have raised, protected and encouraged you for so many years till now. Life is not like that. You need to reflect upon your way of life, how you move from one emotional extreme to another.

While it is of course important to believe that humans are the children of Buddha, children of God, it is also necessary to accept, to a certain extent, the fact that humans are imperfect creatures. As long as we live in this world, as long as we live in a human body, there is always some degree of imperfection.

In this world, it is impossible to live as a perfect being in spiritual terms. You must endure many difficulties that you cannot prevent, so you can only live in an imperfect manner. For this reason you sometimes experience failures and setbacks, but that is exactly when you can find room for self-reflection and opportunity to learn lessons. The same is true for other people; they also experience failures and setbacks, but gain new lessons and recover, thereby trying to lead better lives.

## Accepting awkwardness

What is important is trying to live a better life, not a perfect life. You must tell this to your mind.

However, by saying this I am not suggesting that you can study half-heartedly or work in a disorderly fashion. When I say, "You do not have to live a complete or perfect life," some people may take too lenient an attitude believing that it is alright if their work is not the best they can do and act on that assumption, only to be reprimanded by their boss afterward. They may then get depressed and feel the urge to commit suicide. So, to prevent this from happening I would like to make it quite clear that I am not recommending that one studies or works in a lax manner.

But if any of you are suffering remorse in your soul, severely blaming yourself for some reason to the extent that you are unable to sleep at nights, I want to tell you that you should not strive just for perfection. Eighty percent perfection is fine; somehow try to get through this difficult time. It is important to choose a better life, rather than a complete and perfect life, a life without fault or blemish.

While you are aiming to develop spiritually toward Buddha or God, you are not a Buddha or God Himself. As long as you live in this world, you cannot avoid making mistakes every day and experience suffering. So you should aim to live a better life.

While we humans are the children of Buddha and God, we are imperfect, awkward creatures in this world. We should know this and accept ourselves as struggling to live. You are allowed to be like that since you are currently undergoing soul training and are studying in the school of the soul. It is important that you bear your imperfection and nurture a forgiving heart.

# 2
# Bearing the Suffering
# Caused by a Crime or Accident

## In the case of an uncontrollable event

In the course of life, various incidents or accidents that are beyond our control may occur. There can be for instance, an incident where a teenager murders someone. We can only wonder what made him do what he did, and what his family has to go through.

Society is quick to condemn this kind of juvenile crime. The shame could be too much for the boy's family to bear and some in this situation may even commit suicide. While this may be an example of a "suicide for the sake of honor" that I mentioned in the last section, it is quite common for a parent to become unable to face the neighbors and finally to decide to take his or her own life. This is indeed a painful situation. But these kinds of events that seem beyond human control can happen in life, and the question is how to overcome such a difficulty.

I remember hearing the following story when I was young. A young couple, who had been sweethearts since high school, got married and went to Hawaii on their honeymoon. During their stay, one day the husband went down to the hotel bar for a drink, while his wife remained in the hotel room, probably because she wanted to tidy up. When the husband returned about an hour later, his wife was weeping bitterly. He asked her what was wrong, and she told him that some strangers had forced their way into the room and raped her. They promised each other to keep the incident secret, and returned to Japan.

However, when their first child was born the following year, it had distinctly foreign features and it became impossible for them to keep their secret any longer. It was a true tragedy. In the end, the woman committed suicide by throwing herself into a river. I remember that even as a child, this story left me with a sense of helplessness.

In this case, the husband was inattentive for having left his new bride alone in the room to go drinking on his own. He was to be blamed on this point. Then how about the wife? It being her first time to Hawaii when the foreigners suddenly burst into her room she might not have known what to do and was unable to resist. Moreover, she gave birth to a child with a different colored skin, which added to the tragedy.

Is it actually possible to bear this kind of difficulty in life? This is really a difficult issue. In the end, the wife decided to take her own life, but put yourself in this situation. You, too, would probably find it difficult to continue living.

The couple could have put the infant in an orphanage and carried on their lives as before, or they could have left their hometown to live in some other place where no one knew them. They could even have chosen to get a divorce. In this way there were other alternatives they could have chosen, but there is no denying that it was a very painful situation to overcome.

There was of course an earthly cause for that incident. The couple was actually careless and ignorant about safety. In those days Japanese people were not familiar with overseas travel, so perhaps it would have been better for them if they had just traveled somewhere within Japan like other newlyweds. If they had done this, the tragedy would not have occurred. But they had gone someplace they knew nothing about and the husband had been completely unprotective. Unexpected factors coincided to result in this tragic event.

The question is whether you would be able to carry on living while bearing such shame. The more you think about it, the more you will realize the seriousness of the situation.

## In the case of a traffic accident Caused by carelessness

Many traffic accidents can also be the result of inattentive behavior. Drivers do not usually cause accidents with the clear intention of killing someone. In most cases they hit someone as the result of a momentary lapse of attention. However, even in such cases they face a huge problem.

For instance, a long-distance truck driver may have driven through the night and momentarily nod off when it starts to dawn. Then just at that moment he hits a person and kills him or her. Such an accident can happen. Even though it is the result of just one moment's inattention, if it costs another his life, the driver has to bear this wrong for the rest of his life.

If this happened to you, what would you do? Would you give in to despair? Would you become desperate and commit suicide? You might have to consider changing your job, and worry about what would happen to your family. Many other problems would also arise. You would be tested for your ability to carry on in life while bearing much anguish.

The fact is that you caused an accident because you fell asleep at the wheel, but there is any number of excuses you could make. You could say that anyone would fall asleep if they had to drive the same long distances at night, that you were extremely exhausted, or that the person who died was careless as well. However, even if it were true that the victim had some fault, if you had killed someone, it would be difficult for you to forgive yourself. The test is how you continue your life after such a tragedy.

# 3

## Begin Afresh
## With a Strategy of Withdrawal

### Small and medium-sized businesses
### Are easily disrupted by economic shocks

Recently, the number of company bankruptcies has increased significantly [at the time of the lecture] and there is a strong correlation between bankruptcy and suicide.

During the period of the so-called "bubble economy" in Japan, it was easy to do business, with the rapid increases in profits. As a result, the owners of small businesses employing ten to twenty people, or medium-sized businesses having a staff of between fifty and a hundred, all took large salaries and lived prosperously. In addition to their wages, they also benefited from inflated entertainment allowances, drove luxury imported cars and went out drinking at exclusive clubs, where they give the female hospitality staff expensive presents and spent money lavishly.

Then, however, the economy suddenly collapsed. The proprietors of these small and medium-sized companies had never expected that they would suffer direct damage, particularly when work was connected to the government. Large businesses may have made some preparations, but smaller companies were incapable of planning for such scenarios and the sudden change in the economy threw them into the turbulence.

Their previous optimism disappeared and they bore down to work harder, but they were unable to change their extravagant lifestyles so quickly. They struggled to increase their profits, but due to the recession, there was not much they could do. They tried to get their suppliers to lower their prices, but these companies were in the same situation and rejected such requests because that would cause their own companies to go under. They thought of laying off their employees, but during the good times, they had promised them lifetime employment, so even that option was not open to them. They became gradually pushed into a corner.

## Desperate company owners

When companies were faced with financial difficulties, none of the banks were willing to lend them money. During the boom years the banks had fallen over themselves to lend money, begging them to borrow money to buy land even if they did not need it, but once the bubble burst, the banks would not lend anything, no matter how earnestly the customer asked. The banks acted like someone who would happily lend people umbrellas when the weather was fine, but then demanded them back as soon as it started to rain. This situation actually occurred throughout Japan.

Having no other alternative, small business owners would then use a kind of shadow banking system that would lend money without collateral. It is not difficult to imagine what kind of business would lend money to a company in financial difficulty: the type that charged high interest rates and had organized crime or underworld connections to ensure they got their money back. However, even though these loans allowed the company proprietors to keep their heads above water, this situation could not last long, and as their debts grew it became increasingly difficult for them to repay these loan.

Once this happened the loan sharks started to close in to demand their money back, indicating that it would be pointless to call the police because they would not intervene in civil matters. They would threaten, "You knew what you were getting into when you borrowed the money, now hurry up and pay us back." They would even send people around to the business owner's parents-in-law, demanding that they pay the money. Loan collection thugs would appear everywhere, demanding money every day. Eventually, the borrowers would find themselves forced into a corner unable to see a way out.

Some would then abscond in the middle of the night with their entire families. However, wherever they went they would soon be discovered and all that remained for the business owner was to commit suicide so that their families could claim the money from their life insurance. This kind of suicide is very common among small business owners. But if beneficiaries of the life insurance policy were not clearly specified, the money could be claimed by the creditors, instead of going to the wife and children.

In this kind of situation, they should not think of running away or saving face; they should discuss their situation with a lawyer and declare bankruptcy. Once they have filed for bankruptcy protection and determined the total amount of debt, there is always something that can be done. But by trying to run away, they would only make matters worse. As they were well aware they were indebted, they could not escape the extortion or threats of the thuggish people even if they wanted to.

Basically, it would be quite true to say that it was their own fault that they found themselves in the situation; they were too optimistic of their business potential and borrowed money when they knew it was questionable they would be able to repay it.


## Without an exit strategy the damage will increase

In this way, some people are forced to run off in the night or driven to suicide but it is only because they did not have a strategy to pull back before things reached a critical stage. Some company presidents are unable to pull back because they are simply not aware that running a business during deflation is different from running a business in boom times. They were only familiar with success, which increased the damage even more. Even if they may have knowledge for an exit strategy, closing a business is extremely difficult.

When creditors that one deals with are gangsters, it is almost impossible to rationally explain things to them. People like this are extremely shrewd and are quick to point out conflicting statements a person has made or gaps in memory or logic to intimidate them. No matter how logically or rationally a person may behave, gangsters will always find some fault and pick a fight so the only way to deal with them is in an irrational way.

A book written in the Edo period [1603 – 1867] explained how to deal with creditors when they came to collect on debts at the end of the year. One suggested technique was to grab a chicken by the neck when they visit, make the bird squawk, then cut its head off. This would scare the creditors and cause them to withdraw. A similar method can also work today and that would be for the wife to pretend that she is suffering an emotional breakdown. If she screams at them to go away, throws things and acts in a crazy way, the gangsters would most likely leave. Apparently this method is effective. But she has to be really convincing for it to work; she has to make them believe that she really has gone mad.

Coming back to the point, there are actually many company presidents whose debts drive them to suicide.

Surprisingly, society treats them quite coldly. When a business was doing well the owner behaved in a boastful and selfish manner, thinking they could buy anything they wanted, so when their business crashed, observers would often think that they were getting what they deserved. In such times, the owners need to look back on their past thoughts and actions.

Many of them have never given much thought to a business pullback or how to settle their affairs, so they often bring unforeseen misery upon themselves. What they have to do is put their pride aside, develop their best exit strategy, and think of ways to start afresh. They find themselves in the situation they are in because they could not do anything in advance to prevent it. But they should not quickly choose suicide as their only way out; they must endure a little longer and consider how to overcome the situation.

The worst thing they can do is to borrow more money. They must resist doing this and think of closing down their company instead. It is because they try to save their company at any cost that they end up borrowing money from loan sharks, and then find themselves in trouble, being unable to repay. But once they decide to close their company, they will find that a new life path will open up for them.

There are quite a number of people in this world who have managed to achieve success after their first company went bankrupt, as well as those who have experienced bankruptcy several times before finally achieving success. There are also people who, after having experienced bankruptcy once, have given up the dream of running their own company and instead secured a steady office job. There are many different ways of living. The important point is to avoid being driven by desperation, thereby making the situation even worse.

So do not risk everything on a desperate gamble; instead, consider how to keep the damage to a minimum and how to survive the bad times. The first thing to do is think about protecting yourself and your family; that is important. There are men who choose to die rather than lose face. Women may commit suicide because of problems in the home, but men do it because they are worried about losing face, or because their pride in their position as a company president will not permit them to consider any other alternative.

## Natural selection cannot be avoided In a capitalist society

Businesses are created and closed down in endless cycles. This is something that cannot be avoided in a capitalist society, and eventual business closings are preordained. All kinds of companies are created and then close through a process of natural selection.

Viewed with an objective eye, it is true that badly run companies will disappear while good ones remain. Even in a recession, good companies will prosper. While I understand that no one wants to admit that his or her company was driven to close because it was not run well, seen from a wider perspective, a bankruptcy means that it does fall into "bad" category.

If the word "bad" is inappropriate, I could say it was as "weak" or "uncompetitive." Or it could have been the result of sloppy management. If a company's products are inferior or management is slack, it will be grouped with those that are destined for bankruptcy.

This is unavoidable in a capitalist society. Good companies prosper and as a result, their customers will be able to receive a good service or acquire good products at a good price. Seen from a wider perspective, this is what allows the society to prosper. Seen at the individual business level, however, it can be your company that will go under from constant competition. This might be hard to bear, but if you are lacking in business ability or insight, this is the fate that awaits you.

## As long as you are alive you can always start again

Once things have become hopeless, it is important to consider the best way to dissolve the company. If this is done smoothly there will be no need to commit suicide, but if the owner fails to properly shut down his business, it can result in his suicide or even that of his whole family.

For this reason you must not think only of success, but also consider an exit strategy when things go badly for you. It is important to keep the damage as small as possible. If you get out of the business and have been able to keep the damage to a minimum, you will be able to rebuild your strength for another try, but if you fall short in this, your losses may be total.

Looking at Japanese history, even Nobunaga Oda, the famous 16th-century feudal lord who tried to unify Japan, fled from battle when he realized he could not win. A clan leader he considered his ally, Nagamasa Azai, betrayed him by joining forces with his enemy Yoshikage Asakura. Being unexpectedly attacked on two sides and seeing no hope of victory, Nobunaga retreated, barely escaping with his life, back to his base in Kyoto.

He did not stay and fight to save face. If all he had wanted was a reputation as a great general, a mighty samurai warrior, he would have continued to fight no matter what the odds. Even though his forces were outnumbered two to one, or even though he had been betrayed, he would have continued fighting, but he did not. As soon as he realized he could not win, he retreated home.

There is no such thing as a successful general who does not know when to retreat. Achieving victory when the odds are favorable and retreating in a skillful way when loss is most likely—this is the way to achieve long-continued success.

The same can be said of management. Sometimes you win and sometimes you lose but the important thing when you are losing is how well you cut your losses and rebuild your business.

There are business owners who feel a responsibility for people who have been employed with them for many years, so they take out new loans in an effort to keep their company in business. However, rather than doing this, they could think of ways to retain about eighty percent of the employees, if not all of them.

What can be done to protect the eighty percent? There must be unprofitable sections that could be shut down, or products that could be dropped. There must be some debt that can be repaid. In this way they should focus on trying to ensure that eighty percent of their employees can remain on the job. But if they try to look after everyone, there will sometimes be no alternative but to go bankrupt.

Use all your wisdom to plan a strategy to pull back; otherwise you will simply be fighting a losing battle that in the end could drive you to suicide. You need to use worldly knowledge in all places where applicable.

You should not prematurely think that you will just end your life when all else fails. Life is life because you are living and as long as you are alive, you can always get back on your feet again. No matter how many times you failed in the past, you can always recover.

If you are considering committing suicide and maybe even taking your whole family with you, surely there must be other actions that can be done before that. From this perspective you will see there is always something that can be done. Before you reach the point where death seems to be the only option, there will be any number of things that you can give up or different actions that you could take. After doing everything you can, you should retreat.

## Consider the odds in love and exams

Not only company presidents commit suicide as a result of losing face or of wounds to their pride. There are also people who commit suicide after having failed in love. In most cases they are people who wanted to marry someone beyond their reach. However, even in the matters of love, you should consider what your chances for success will be.

Of course, there are some who succeed in marrying film stars, but it is very unlikely that this will happen to you. If you wish to marry a film star, you will have one or two thousand rivals and the odds will be against you. Even if the object of your desire is not so well-known, a relationship is not always easy to achieve.

Therefore, in the case of love, too, it is necessary to objectively estimate your odds of success. If you are a woman, look at the man of your choice and ask yourself, "What is the chance of a woman like me marrying a man with his looks, income and position?" It is sad, but this is something that must be done. You have to be quite objective and ask if you have a more than a fifty percent chance, more than an eighty percent chance or, on the other hand whether your chances are only twenty or thirty percent.

You can make as much effort as you can, but there will be a point beyond which further effort would be wasted. You must recognize this point and once you go beyond this limit you need to decide to give up. There will definitely be someone else well suited for you.

Some level of interaction can be achieved through effort, but anything beyond that will be an attachment that will make you suffer, because the other party may have different plans or hopes of his or her own. You should not marry a person at the cost of his or her happiness so you must give up at a certain point.

When figuring out your possibilities of getting together with another person, you need to consider how much effort you need to put in and determine whether or not the other will accept you. If you recognize it is impossible, you should withdraw and look for another potential partner.

You will always find another opportunity for marriage. Someone new is sure to turn up in a year or two. The object of your current interest is not necessarily your last chance in life. There are people in this world who marry in their seventies, so there is absolutely no reason to take any premature action in your twenties. Try to think about matters of love in this way, considering the odds for and against success.

You may also fail an exam. But in taking exams too, consider the odds of success, bearing in mind that failure is always a possible outcome. When you fail, it is important that you are prepared to do better the next time, to aim for an opportunity to turn your life around.

# 4

# The Courage to Forgive Yourself

## What is necessary when fighting a losing battle?

I have spoken about worldly wisdom. You need to know the way to live through this life and use all the wisdom at your disposal. However, no matter how great your command of wisdom might be, there are sometimes obstacles that are impossible to overcome. For instance, although you might be eager to become prime minister of a country, there is very little likelihood of your achieving this aim. If you look at the odds, you will realize that they are more than a thousand to one, or even more than ten thousand to one.

This is not to say that a prime minister is smarter than you; that is not necessarily the case. While this is mysterious, the people who become prime ministers do so because they are fated to do so. In the same way, people who do not have the fate will not become prime minister, however much they may want to. Their ambitions will most likely be thwarted. Or if you want to become an emperor, you will have to start a revolution and it is more likely you will receive the death penalty than achieve your dream.

When facing a challenge, you will of course need to consider the situation calmly, fight with all the talents available to you in this world and strive to win, but sometimes you may be unable to win and find yourself fighting a losing battle. At such times, your ability to continue standing firm and to endure the situation is very important.

What is needed when you have not been able to achieve your goal and have failed despite all your best efforts and wisdom? It is courage, the courage to forgive yourself. You may want to reproach yourself, saying that you are no good, you are a failure, but you need to have the courage to forgive yourself in defeat. Tell yourself that you did your best, you tried your hardest, that although you couldn't achieve your goal, it was beyond your control. You need the strength and courage to forgive yourself in this way.

When you have unfortunately failed to achieve success despite having done your utmost, to the best of your ability, you need the courage to put away your "weapons" with good grace and admit defeat. While it is quite painful to concede that you have lost, you need the courage to do so. At such times, the power of self-forgiveness will come forth.

## Set a time limit on mental suffering

There are people who continue to suffer from failure for ten or twenty years, being unable to forgive themselves. During the course of their lives, people experience all kinds of failures—involving human relations, work, business, or the opposite sex. Many people experience suffering in their lives and there are as many sorrows, failures and broken hopes in this world as there are people. It is sad, but unfortunately not everyone can succeed because in many cases, one person's success is another person's failure.

When you fail, it is foolish to suffer endlessly. You need to reflect on the areas that require reflection, apologize where necessary, recognize any mistakes you may have made, and decide not to repeat the same mistakes again. Nevertheless, it is utterly foolish to suffer for longer than necessary.

In both the civil and criminal law of Japan, there is a system called the statute of limitations, which states that a person cannot be tried for a crime after a set period of time has elapsed. One reason for this is technical. For example, after several years, the relationship between what is to be gained or lost will become unclear, or the evidence becomes obscure or irrelevant.

Another reason is that people's memories and emotions will fade with time. For instance, if a civil case were to be brought to reclaim a loan that was decades old, it would be difficult to prove whether the loan had actually been made; the relationship between creditor and debtor has become unclear and people's memories would have become faint. On top of that, a creditor demanding money back after ten or twenty years could simply mean that it was insignificant to him.

In the case of murder, if someone makes an accusation many years after the event, the evidence and people connected to the case may no longer be available for trial and the details of the case will have become unclear. In addition to this, the emotions of hate and fear will also have weakened somewhat. It is for these reasons that the statute of limitations exists.

If a time limit exists in law, it should also exist in the mind, in your own mind. So, tell yourself, "I have already suffered enough for that mistake. Three years have passed now so it is about time for me to forgive myself."

# 5

# The Courage to Forgive Others

## Do not continue to hate others

There are people who are determined to hate specific persons for their entire lives, but after a certain time has passed, they should realize that hating so much will only cause thems pain. It is essential to decide to forgive the person.

If you have hate in your heart, you will most likely feel physically unwell. The person who is the object of your dislike will feel bad, but so will you.

Many people who suffer from mysterious illnesses often hold strong feelings of hatred. If you cannot forgive a person for something and form a strong hatred for him or her, through neurobiological processes this hatred can create some malformation inside your body. Destructive emotions or hatred may sometimes materialize as cancerous cells. In this way, illness can be generated from the most unexpected sources.

Therefore, you must forgive others for your own sake as well. While it is necessary to forgive yourself, you must also forgive others.

There may certainly be many people who have harmed you, embarrassed you, persecuted or insulted you, but you must forgive them. Surely it is enough for you to suffer for one year, three years or five years.

The people you hate may well have changed with the passage of time; they may regret what they did to you. They may think, "I insulted him at the time, but now I am sorry I did so." Perhaps someone made fun of you for having a religious belief but three years later, the very same person who mocked you may now be a religious believer himself. People can change in this way so you should not hold on to your hatred. Even if someone may have treated you badly and brought you pain, do not continue to hate him or her; instead, tell yourself that the other person is also an imperfect human being.

## Place a time limit on unforgiveness as well

Let me tell you about this case from real life. There was a man who opened a chain of restaurants and became very successful. He wrote a book about his experiences and although he had confidence in himself, he still retained feelings of unforgiveness over an event that happened when he was completing elementary school.

He wrote, "I was very clever as a boy and was even compared to the renowned Buddhist monk, Kukai [774 – 835, founder of the Shingon Sect of Buddhism], but when I applied to enter middle school, I was turned down. I later discovered that in my elementary school file record my homeroom teacher had written, 'This student should not be accepted'."

Apparently this teacher gave good recommendations to pupils whose parents had treated him with seasonal gifts but the mother of the man in question was a woman of integrity who refused to give any special treatment and did not give the teacher any gifts. As a result, the teacher had written negative remarks in the recommendation and the middle school had accepted the teacher's words without question. Students with worse academic records than his were accepted into the middle school, while the future restaurant owner was forced to take his sixth year of elementary school again at a different school before being accepted one year later.

Decades had passed since the event, but he still had included it in his biography so he must have been quite affected by it. This experience probably provided him with the motivation to succeed later in life, but it seems that no matter how many years had passed, he could not forgive the outrageous behavior of his teacher.

This person was probably simply unfortunate in that he and his teacher did not get along. The teacher was doubtless a weak man who was willing to give good recommendations to those students whose families gave him seasonal gifts but spiteful towards those who did not. He may have assumed that the student did not like him. That is why, when this student tried to get into middle school on ability alone, he acted pettily and purposely put bad comments in the student's record. This action outraged the former student, who found out about it many years later.

The young boy was later successful in business and became a rich man, so we could say that this experience had pushed him to study harder and ultimately brought him good results. Even so, no matter how many decades had passed, he seemed unable to forget the vexation he experienced at the time.

In this way, failure, insult, scorn and persecution can inspire people to try harder and act as a major turning point in their life, but after a certain number of years, a statute of limitations should be applied to such matters as well. Otherwise, feelings of hate and resentment will linger in your mind, making you give off a hellish vibration, which is not a good thing. You can decide for yourself how long you will hold onto your feelings of unforgiveness, but after a set period of time, make up your mind to forgive yourself, or the person who wronged you.

# 6

## Mistakes Are Also Valuable Experiences

In ancient China, when a general had lost in battle, he was not permitted to surrender. If he did and returned home, not only he, but also his whole family would be put to death. This practice continued for a long time. That is why, when the Han Dynasty General Li Ling was defeated in battle against the Xiongnu, a nomadic steppe people around 100 B.C., he then defected to fight against the Chinese empire. In this way, there were kingdoms where military leaders would be sentenced to death or exiled if defeated in battle.

In ancient Rome, on the other hand, a defeated general would be called back and then, after a period of rehabilitation, would be sent out to lead another army several years later. This was the secret of Rome's great military strength.

The logic behind this was that someone who had once been defeated would learn from the experience concerning which tactics had led to his loss. A leader who was new to battle might make the same mistakes as the person he was replacing so the Roman method was to send in a man who had experienced defeat earlier in his career. In this way, even if a general had been defeated, after a certain period he could be given a leadership role over and over again.

Someone who has never commanded an army before may well make common mistakes but a person who had experienced defeat would have learned from it and gained wisdom each time. He would understand what had led to his defeat and Roman policy was to not let this knowledge waste. This is an example of a democratic idea being applied in a military context.

In Japanese politics today, we sometimes see politicians who have served as ministers losing their cabinet posts to return to being regular members of the Diet, then getting reinstated to the cabinet in the next administration. We also see that the party in power changes several times. This is an example of the Roman thinking that underlies modern democratic politics. No matter how many times a politician may fail, he or she can return to power after collecting a greater store of experience. This is an example of the principle of the forgiveness of sins included in a political system.

In the workplace, too, good work is generally rewarded and bad work is punished, but we need to know that within certain limits, the power to forgive can increase the strength of a company. There are very few people able to go through their entire career without making a single mistake; in fact, in many cases those who have never made a mistake are those who have never really done any work.

People who do not work will not make mistakes. On the other hand, the more boldly a person works, the more mistakes he or she will make.

Of course, if people who make mistakes are not given any kind of reprimand, it will lower the morale of the entire company, so it is right that good work should be rewarded while bad work is punished. However, the experience of failure can also be nourishment for the soul so it is important that after a certain period has passed, the person who failed is given a second chance.

If "the forgiveness of sin" is included in the work ethic, we become able to regard mistakes as valuable experiences too. This idea is beneficial not only for the individuals but also for the entire organization; viewing and treating employees in this way will often result in stronger performance in the workplace as a whole.

# 7

# Try to Achieve a Turnaround Within Your Lifetime

I have looked at the power to forgive sins from various perspectives. What I wish to say can be summed up as follows:

In general, life in this world only lasts decades, though some people may live up to a hundred and twenty years old. After death, even though you may wish to be reincarnated soon, it cannot be done so quickly. You came into this world because of your repeated pleas to do so. This being the case, once you have succeeded in being born, do not try to hurry to your death. Everyone is eventually doomed to die, and your time will also come one day. So it is worthwhile to try and achieve a turnaround in the time that remains to you. Do your best in your given circumstances, for you will never have the same chance again.

In order to do so, it is best not to be too much of a perfectionist. Accept the imperfections that come with humanity, what can be called the animalistic part of your being. You and those around you share this animalistic aspect of human character; that is why you are sometimes at the mercy of emotions and feel anger, lament, cry out, make a blunder, feel victimized, or become aggressive to others.

All humans have this kind of imperfect inclination, and it is because of this that you still have much to learn in your soul training. Please be aware of this, and accept the imperfections of being human.

Blaming yourself too much for your sins will sometimes lead you to commit another and greater wrong. People who seek too much perfection may often commit another great sin.

Failure in business is quite common. During such times, your pride may stop you from knowing when to draw back and you may remain obstinate in your position, leading you to greater downfall. It may then result not only in suffering for you, but also for your family. But it is possible to find a way to avoid this.

Therefore, do not fight for the sake of your honor or pride alone, rather think calmly to find an appropriate approach. Use every bit of wisdom you possess to solve the problems that can be solved with earthly wisdom.

When wisdom falls short, what is needed is courage. You need courage to forgive yourself and you need courage to forgive others. Having courage is essential.

# 8
## Believe in a World
## That Transcends the Rational

### The mysticism of religion

When it comes to courage, I believe that religion has great power. Two thousand years have passed since Christianity began and to a large extent, it has been veiled in mythology. Contemporary people have only a vague understanding of the Bible and think that the wonders it describes as being merely symbolic. They rarely discuss them in depth.

For instance, the Bible describes how the Virgin Mary gave birth to Jesus, and this event has been described as a miracle. I would like to consider this point.

Today, it is not unusual to witness young brides walking down the aisle for marriage who are noticeably pregnant. There are some whose pregnancies are so advanced that they are unable to go on a honeymoon. It would be safe to conclude that the same type of situation happened two thousand years ago, that Mary became pregnant before marriage. It was nothing extraordinary.

For two thousand years, however, Christianity has insisted that this was a case of "Immaculate Conception." Standing firmly on this, they have developed their own particular logic and the story has become a mystical aspect of Christian religions. According to their belief, Jesus was not born of the coupling between a man and a woman. He was not a mere human with a physical body, but had the Holy Spirit dwelling in him. This developed into the mystical explanation that the Holy Spirit came down to be born as Jesus Christ. It is certainly true that a Holy Spirit, or soul, resided in his human body. Furthermore, this idea developed into meaning that Jesus was born free of sin, that he was without blemish. In worldly terms this may seem somewhat improbable but symbolically it makes good sense.

What about Jesus Christ himself? Jesus gave teachings and had twelve main disciples. Eventually, hundreds even thousands of common people followed him. However, after only three years of preaching he was arrested and crucified alongside criminals.

His disciples believed that even as he was dying on the cross, an angel would come to save him, that there would be one final miracle. So they watched and waited. But Jesus died, without any miracle happening, no one came to save him. He simply died with a crown of thorns on his head. This was shocking to his disciples.

The confused disciples dispersed, but eventually began to assert that the man who had died on a cross like a criminal was actually the Savior, that Jesus had risen from the dead. They established this faith and stood by this belief no matter what happened. Then eventually, it came to be accepted as the truth.

In terms of the soul, the story of Christ's resurrection is true; even though the body may have died, the soul lived on. Even though he may have been put to death as a criminal on earth, in the heavenly realm his soul was resurrected as a great being. This is what the story of the resurrection symbolizes.

From how it is written in the Bible, we might imagine that he resurrected physically as if some kind of zombie. That is the way the story is told. But this is somewhat extreme and far from the truth. The Bible promotes this ideology of resurrection and uses it to support the belief in the Savior. Although what happened was the exact opposite of their assertion, the disciples developed this idea of faith and pushed it forward. As they repeatedly told this story as truth, it was gradually accepted as so. It is strange, but this happens in the world of religion.

### "I believe because it is irrational"

Religion is not something you believe in because it is rational. To believe in something that is rational is a matter of course, and everyone does this regularly. For instance, buying a quality product recommended by a friend at the lowest price would be a rational act. It is a natural function of economics. But religion and faith are different.

Religion has an aspect that is extremely irrational. There is a part of every religion that demands people believe in it because it is irrational. Only when people build their faith despite irrationality will a religion survive beyond the change of time.

Standards of rationality change over time and what is accepted today will be entirely different in fifty, one hundred or two hundred years' time. In economic terms, even if one may find a good cheap product, cheaper ones will soon come along. Even if one may find the best color television, more advanced sets will eventually be produced. People once thought that public telephones were indispensable but now they have been largely replaced by mobile phones.

We live in a rapidly changing society and things that were said to be "the very best" have continued to improve. For this reason we cannot rely on the choices or decisions that are made solely according to the current logic of this world. Believing in such factors is not a religious belief.

The world of religion is an eternal world, an imperishable world, where there are everlasting truths. There is an aspect in the world of religion that demands that people say, "I believe despite its irrationality," "I believe because it is absurd." Within this irrationality is something that is actually symbolic. There are symbolic truths that transcend the physical or material things, or earthly matters. When everyone starts to believe in these symbolic truths, they become imperishable.

To live a better life in this world, it is important to have rational thoughts, to make rational decisions and act

in a rational way. You cannot live to your full potential in this world unless you are strong in a worldly
way. However, as long as people remain in the earthly
domain, religions can never be found. Belief in something
that transcends this earthly perspective and transcends
rationality is indispensable in religion. That "something"
is actually the eternal Truth.

Christianity is two thousand years old. It was
founded around the start of the Yayoi Era in Japanese
history. Buddhism is two thousand five hundred years
old, founded during the Jomon Era when people mainly
used earthenware and still relied on stone tools. Can
people today really believe in the teachings of people
who lived in such ancient times? Can the teachings of
those times make really sense today? Viewed rationally
from a worldly perspective, they are almost entirely
irrelevant. However, the symbolic part of the teachings
has universal strength, an imperishable power. Unless
people can see these aspects in the teachings, religion
has not formed.

This can be said of Happy Science as well. Today
Happy Science is an extremely influential religion with
unique characteristics. It has power while at the same time
it is rational. However, if that was all it possessed, if it did
not have more beyond that, then it would not embody the
imperishability of a true religion.

There are many strange religions in the world
today but there are tens of thousands, even hundreds

of thousands of people who believe in them. Some religions may contain elements that cannot be perceived from a worldly perspective. Even in those religions that are regarded as misleading, they may well have certain aspects that actually express religious truth. If we denied these altogether, then we would not be able to see the true essence of religion.

Even major religions were often targets of persecution in their initial stages. This treatment happened because in many cases the Truth does not accord with the reality or rational thinking of this world. So it is necessary for more and more people to believe in the Truth that transcends rationality.

To say that you believe in something because it is rational is the same as saying you use a mobile telephone because it is convenient. If the membership of a religion is only made up of people who say, "This religion is convenient and useful, so I will make use of it," "It benefits me in many ways and that's why I believe in it," then that religion will not last very long. It will experience the same situation as in Jesus' time when his disciples became unable to believe in him upon seeing him die on the cross.

So, believe in a world that goes beyond mere rationality. People who believe in a religion and live by its teachings must strive to perceive what is beyond rationality.

I have talked about a variety of topics. If you are able to understand the power of forgiving sins from different angles, I will be happy.

Chapter Three

# WORK ABILITY AND ENLIGHTENMENT

## *How to Become a Person Who Can Bring Happiness to Many*

# 1

## Shakyamuni Buddha Was Highly Competent at Work As Well

### Shakyamuni Buddha's spiritual discipline And missionary work

In this chapter, I would like to cover the topic of, "Work Ability and Enlightenment." I have chosen this subject because people tend to think that work competence is an important ability for lay people, while enlightenment is the special domain of priests. I often feel that people tend to separate these two abilities.

A separation of this kind will provide people with a way to make excuses. Those who are not very skilled at work tend to believe that they possess a higher level of enlightenment, while people who have not achieved a high level of enlightenment tend to believe that they are better at their jobs. I have the feeling that this sort of thinking allows people to make excuses for themselves in either way. Therefore, I would like to consider this problem in greater depth.

It is possible to achieve enlightenment by undergoing spiritual discipline in solitary isolation in mountains or in a cave. In Buddhism, someone who has achieved enlightenment in this way is called *Pratyekabuddha* [a lone buddha] or self-enlightened one. This type of practitioner does not study under a master or train with others, but prefers to go into mountain forests and find enlightenment on his or her own.

Among these hermits, there may be some who could attain eminence as mountain saints. But these sorts of practitioners do not go beyond the level of self-enlightenment and do not have any influence on other people. They train alone and die alone. They may or may not have attained enlightenment. As they have no contact with the outside world, their enlightenment does not go beyond the level of self-fulfillment. Some of them may indeed have attained an extremely high level of enlightenment but no one will ever know. Even if they claim to have attained enlightenment in a mountain cave, no one would have seen or heard of them so they would have had no influence on anyone.

These people, who claim to have become enlightened without any interaction with others, may believe that they had reached a high level of enlightenment but, in fact, their enlightenment is often self-conceit. While the Buddhist saying, "Holy am I alone," is usually spoken of in a positive way, those who claim to have attained enlightenment on their own tend to use this concept in a worldly way and believe that they should be uniquely revered. But the truth is that their claim is often egocentric and their enlightenment does not serve any good. You must be careful not to fall into a trap like this.

Shakyamuni Buddha spent almost six years practicing this form of solitary training, but after he attained his great enlightenment, he was very enthusiastic to convey this enlightenment to others. He organized a group of followers to manifest his enthusiasm in a tangible way; this is a hard, historical fact.

While there are different estimates of the number of monks who joined his order, we know definitely that there were over one thousand monks in total. In Buddhist scriptures, it is often stated that he had 1,250 disciples but that was only one method of counting. There were actually different types of monks as well as lay members who lived like monks, so it was actually impossible to determine the exact number. That being said, it is clear at a minimum that there were over a thousand full-time dedicated monks who supported themselves through the receiving of alms. [In Chapter Four of *The Laws of the Sun* (New York: IRH Press, 2018), it is stated that there were more than five thousand disciples in the latter days of the Buddha.]

Life would be difficult if one thousand monks were to live together in one place, so they were spread out at several sites for their training and missionary work. The main centers of training were the Venuvana [Bamboo Grove] Monastery in the Magadha Kingdom, and the Jetavana Monastery in the Kosala Kingdom, and there were several other places besides these. The Buddha and his disciples used these centers to undergo spiritual discipline and as bases from which to engage in missionary work.

The Buddha had certainly focused his efforts on his own training in the early days, but after his great enlightenment he was enthusiastic about teaching and educating large numbers of people. He was certainly very eager to spread the Dharma [Laws] as he continued to undergo spiritual training, and to guide the common people to the path of happiness.

Shakyamuni Buddha, the original teacher of Buddhism, strived to spread the teachings to many people using his groups of followers, in addition to seeking enlightenment on his own. This is an undeniable historical fact. Most certainly he would not remain content spending his whole life living alone in a cave in the mountains.

## Aim to become capable at work
## While increasing your enlightenment

Thus, the Buddhist style of activities was to spread the teachings and guide people by organizational means. This means that its activities would require a considerable amount of worldly work abilities. Therefore, you cannot say that work competence is only important for lay people. It is clear that Shakyamuni Buddha made efforts to create a group of professionally-skilled monks who were well versed in the teachings and well trained, to systematically spread the Truth while still sustaining the group.

If we were to compare Shakyamuni Buddha and Confucius, we would see a clear difference in their style of activities. Confucius traveled to various states in China in search of work in governmental positions, but it was difficult for him to find employment. As a result, his disciples were most always famished and the number of disciples who travelled with him remained small. Confucius was probably incapable of envisioning a systematic plan for missionary work on the scale of Shakyamuni Buddha.

It is true that at the start of his religious training Shakyamuni Buddha acted like an Indian Yogi, retreating to riverbanks and mountains on his own in search of true enlightenment, but he did not turn into an ascetic hermit. This fact is clear. From this we can assume that there is a strong correlation between work competence, Buddhist enlightenment, and the Mahayana movement of salvation. Work competence cannot necessarily be considered as only a lay skill.

This is based on the fact that Shakyamuni Buddha possessed both worldly and unworldly abilities, and that he was actually born the prince of Kapilavastu. Shakyamuni Buddha was raised to be a future king, training in a princely manner until he was twenty-nine years old; it was only a matter of time before he would become king.

He had learned many valuable skills in order to become a king, including how to manage people and issues regarding food, taxes, and the military. For instance, he studied ways to defend his city in case of invasion by one of its neighbors. It is doubtless that he had also studied management in modern terms, while at the same time he was skilled with numbers from a mathematical viewpoint.

Seen from this aspect, I must say that you are making an excuse when you say, "Seeking enlightenment will only lead you to be incompetent at work." In fact, being competent at work while increasing one's level of enlightenment will lead to the salvation of many. If you actually succeed in saving large numbers of people, it is proof that your enlightenment has strong power and universality; it is powerful enough to save many people.

This can be easily understood if you imagine the following case. You may be astonished at seeing an ascetic who seeks solitary enlightenment on a mountain, living on wild nuts and fruits, or who can stand on his hands all day as part of his spiritual training. But his life does not go beyond that level and he has nothing to teach others. I believe that showing each person the way to solve their problems is a far greater task.

Therefore, if you merely think, "Work competence is only an ability necessary for lay believers and enlightenment is a power only required of monks," I must say that your reasoning is too simple and you are simply making excuses for yourself. This point is worth deep contemplation.

# 2
# Enlightenment in Zen Buddhism
# —Shen-hsiu and Hui-neng

## Education is impossible if
## The process of making an effort is neglected

With regard to work ability and enlightenment, it is not sufficient to simply say "enlightenment on its own is not enough, competence at work is also important." I feel very strongly that one's competence at work will also affect the nature of one's personal enlightenment.

For example, the Tientai sect of Buddhism teaches the philosophy of innate Buddha-nature, saying that everyone can become enlightened without effort, but I have criticized this idea [refer to Chapter 12 of *The Challenge of Enlightenment* (London: Little Brown Book Group, 2006), and Chapter 4 of *The Golden Laws* (New York: Lantern Books, 2011)].

Metaphorically speaking, this idea is similar to a school principal telling students on the first day of class, "You are already wonderful people, you are all talented and you will all get the best grades on your exams." Theoretically, you could certainly get high grades if you study hard enough, but in real life things are not so easy; some of your answers will be correct and some will not.

So the most logical way to improve your ability is through continuous study for many years. If this process of effort is ignored, education will be meaningless.

If teachers say to their students, "You are all buddhas, just as you are. You were born as buddhas so there is no need to do more," they are neglecting education altogether and it is no different from saying, "Education is useless." In a sense, this is the same as neglecting discipline and training after birth. Actually, this way of thinking had a strong influence on the form of enlightenment of the Zen sect.

## The enlightenment of Shen-hsiu, the top disciple Of the Fifth Patriarch Hung-jen

Zen is a school of Buddhism started by Bodhidharma, who was active in the late fifth to early sixth centuries and had traveled from India to China. While there were some problems in the teachings of the founder Bodhidharma himself, the Sixth Patriarch Hui-neng [638 – 713 A.D.] who established the Southern sect of Chinese Zen, was even more problematic.

The teacher of the Sixth Patriarch Hui-neng was the Fifth Patriarch Hung-jen [or Hongren][601 – 674 A.D.]. Hung-jen had been teaching disciples for many years, but when he became old, he decided that it was time to look for a successor and retire. Hung-jen's temple was fairly popular and according to one source, it had about seven hundred disciples. [Other sources have said "five hundred" or "more than one thousand."]

Among his elders, the top disciples who assisted him with the instruction of students, was a monk named Shen-hsiu [or Shenxiu][606 – 706 A.D.]. Shen-hsiu was an extremely gifted disciple in his fifties. As he had mastered the teachings sufficiently and had an admirable character, everyone expected him to take over the leadership of the temple.

Nevertheless, the Fifth Patriarch Hung-jen thought that he could not just let Shen-hsiu inherit his temple without some kind of test, so he decided to have a contest for the disciples to describe the enlightenment they had achieved. He asked them all to write of their enlightenment in the form of a gatha, or poem, and post it on a wall.

All the other disciples felt that the assistant teacher, Shen-hsiu, would become the next leader of the temple and if they posted their verses on enlightenment, it would only be distracting, so they did not write anything.

Not one disciple posted a gatha and seeing this, Shen-hsiu humbly wrote of his enlightenment and posted it on the middle of the south corridor wall without signing his name. His gatha read:

The body is the Bodhi tree,
The mind like a clear mirror's stand.
We must constantly strive to wipe it
And must not let it attract dust.

A Bodhi tree is the "tree of enlightenment" in India [*pippala* or *Ashvattha* in Sanskrit], and Shakyamuni Buddha is said to have meditated and achieved great enlightenment under this tree. So, "The body is the Bodhi tree" means "This body of mine is the tree of enlightenment."

"Clear mirror" means a mirror that is unclouded, and you can imagine "a clear mirror's stand" to be a dresser mirror used for makeup. "The mind is like a clear mirror's stand" then means, "The mind is like a gleaming, unblemished mirror's stand." So it says we must make efforts constantly to wipe it clean, so it would not attract any dust, dirt, or grime.

In this gatha, Shen-hsiu meant that the body is like the Bodhi tree, yearning for enlightenment as one lives, while the mind is the Buddha-nature that is like a clear mirror's stand. Therefore, it is important to always be diligent and wipe it clean so it does not attract dust, dirt, or grime.

This is a most orthodox form of Buddhist enlightenment and it certainly accords with the Buddha's teachings, including the Noble Eightfold Path. When the other disciples read this gatha they were most impressed and said, "We knew that Shen-hsiu was the right person, he deserves to be the leading disciple. He is definitely the one to inherit this temple."

On that occasion, however, a man named Hui-neng came forward.

## Hui-neng, the man who succeeded Hung-jen

Hui-neng was from southern China. In those days, a great distinction was made of people from north or south China; it was believed that the north was more civilized while the south was inhabited by barbarians. Apparently, southerners were discriminated against and were considered as not possessing Buddha-nature.

Hui-neng, a native to the south, was very small in stature, and his face was said to resemble a monkey [or in another version of the story, a wolf]. So he was the target of other people's scorn.

Hui-neng had been allowed to study at Hung-jen's temple, but still had not been ordained as a monk. He had yet to have the precepts imparted to him, and was just doing various odd jobs. Although allowed entrance to the temple, he had been pounding rice in the rice mill for eight months without having been taught the rules of priesthood.

This was not simply because he was from the southern part of the country, but also because he could not read or write. For a monk to be unable to read or write was a major obstacle. In modern terms, it was basically equivalent to someone who has not finished elementary school.

Seeing that everyone in the temple was very agitated, he asked his friends what had happened. One of them answered, "One of the elders, Shen-hsiu, has written a gatha summarizing his enlightenment and presented it.

He is sure to be the next head priest of the temple so everyone is very excited."

"What has he written?" Hui-neng asked, "Read it for me."

"It says that the body is the Bodhi tree and the mind is a clear mirror's stand, so we must sometimes wipe it clean so as not to attract dirt and dust. Master Hung-jen also agrees with it, and says that if we do as Shen-hsiu suggests, we cannot go wrong."

At this time Hui-neng was still in his early twenties but when he heard what Shen-hsiu had written, he replied, "That does not sound like much of enlightenment to me."

"What are you talking about, what do you know, you just work pounding rice," his friends said.

Hui-neng then asked him, "I cannot write, so would you write down what I am going to say?" He then produced the following gatha:

Bodhi originally has no tree
The clear mirror also has no stand
Fundamentally there is not a single thing
Where could dust be attracted?
[Or according to the Dunhuang version, the last two lines could be read, "Buddha-nature is always clear and pure; Where is there room for dust?"]

What this gatha means is, "Enlightenment originally has no tree. The clear mirror does not have a stand. Humans essentially possess nothing so where can the dust, dirt, and grime be attracted? There is nowhere."

After he had his friend write this and post it in the corridor, the whole temple was stirred up once again, with people saying, "An amazing person has appeared," or "Something astonishing has happened." A shock wave passed through the temple.

When the teacher Hung-jen saw the poem, he was most impressed, but he knew that if he were to let others know how he felt, it would cause much trouble, so he just commented, "It's nothing special," pretending to ignore it. That night, however, he visited Hui-neng in the rice mill.

Hui-neng was a short man, only about 1.5 meters [five feet] tall, and Hung-jen asked this rice-pounder, "Is the rice ready?" Hui-neng then replied, "The rice has been ready for a long time. It is now waiting for the sieve," meaning, "I have been enlightened to the necessary level, but this enlightenment has yet to be properly recognized." This was the dialogue between the Zen master and the rice pounder.

Upon hearing his answers, the Fifth Patriarch Hung-jen decided to make him his successor, and without saying a word, struck the rice mortar three times with his staff, then left. In the temple, time was told by the beating of a drum and midnight was indicated by three beats of the drum. By striking his staff three times in such a way, he was telling Hui-neng that he should visit him at that time.

When Hui-neng went to Hung-jen's room at the appointed hour, Hung-jen began to teach him the essence of the enlightenment of the Diamond Sutra [it is said that this continued for three days and three nights], then he gave Hui-neng the robe and begging bowl that had been passed down from master to master, originating from Bodhidharma himself.

As he passed these items to Hui-neng, Hung-jen said, "You have inherited the robe and bowl but this will cause many problems. Others will find it hard to forgive you so you should take these and escape." The reason he said this was that Hui-neng had not even officially been accepted into the priesthood at the time. He could not read or write and he was still very young, in his early twenties, about twenty-four years old. [Other accounts give his age as twenty-two, thirty-two, or thirty-four.]

Thereafter Hui-neng planned his escape in the middle of the night using the docks at JiuJiang. Hung-jen then helped him by rowing him across the river and watched as Hui-neng went south to escape.

## The "sudden enlightenment" of Southern Zen And the "gradual enlightenment" of Northern Zen

After that, Hung-jen did not come out to give any sermons to the disciples in the temple, so they visited the master to find out if anything was wrong. To their surprise, however, Hung-jen told them that he had retired. The disciples asked him what this meant and he explained that the robe and bowl that symbolized his office had already been passed on to Hui-neng.

With this news, the temple was thrown into an uproar. "That rice-pounder has taken the robe and bowl and escaped! Shen-hsiu was supposed to become the next master. Master Hung-jen must have lost his mind to give the symbols of office to that rice-pounder. We can't let him get away!" cried the disciples and set out in pursuit of Hui-neng.

Among the disciples was a man named Hui-ming, who had been a general before joining the priesthood, and he went after Hui-neng to bring back the robe and bowl. However, he eventually became converted by Hui-neng and failed to retrieve them.

Hung-jen had told Hui-neng to travel south and live a quiet life in the mountains for about twenty years, so it was some time before he returned to the world. Regarding the length of time he hid in the mountains, there are various accounts of the story, some saying about fifteen years. [Other sources say that the master had told him to hide for three years and that he actually had hidden for three years, while others say five.] When he escaped from the temple he was about twenty-four years old, so he became active when he was in his forties. Then the Southern sect of Zen began.

For his part, Shen-hsiu founded the Northern sect of Zen and it flourished. He gained the respect of three Emperors, including Empress Wu Tse-t'ien, and was even granted the posthumous title, Ta-t'ung Ch'an-shih [meaning Greatly Penetrating Dhyana Master]. Although his sect produced the great masters P'u-chi and I-fu, it did not last for long.

This is how Zen Buddhism became split between the belief in "sudden enlightenment" of the Southern sect and the "gradual enlightenment" of the Northern sect. The "sudden enlightenment" of the south then gained more followers to become the mainstream belief of Chinese Zen. It was this style of Zen that was later introduced into Japan.

# 3

## Problems with Zen
## That Teaches Sudden Enlightenment

### Enlightenment as if walking a fine line
### Between sanity and insanity

The rise of Hui-neng was extremely significant in terms of the history of Buddhism. He indeed was a prominent figure, so I would like to consider his enlightenment further.

The gatha Shen-hsiu wrote was that the body is the Bodhi tree, the tree of enlightenment, and the mind is an unblemished mirror stand that must sometimes be wiped clean to remove dust or dirt. There is no mistake in this statement and it accords with the Buddha's teachings. It is a very orthodox model answer for a student, and a standard, reasonable opinion. Judging from the way in which the Northern sect was to prosper, there can be no doubt that Shen-hsiu was certainly a highly competent person.

On the other hand, what was it that Hui-neng spoke of in his gatha, "Originally Bodhi has no tree, the clear mirror has no stand"? Judging from the later development of Buddhism, it can be interpreted as the philosophy of "void," which states: "All things of this world are non-substantial. In other words, everything that exists in this world is void. Essentially nothing exists in this world;

physical bodies do not exist and material things do not exist. All things are void." If we interpret this idea as a way of thinking to rid ourselves of all attachments of this world, we can certainly say it is an enlightenment that has tremendous power.

However, this enlightenment of void will lead to a problem that is unique to Zen, like balancing on the border between sanity and insanity, or metaphorically speaking walking on a fence; if you fall on the right, you will stay sane, but if you fall to the left, you will become insane.

If you interpret this gatha as expressing the state of void, where you have abandoned all worldly attachments, then it can be highly effective. However, if someone who has not yet achieved this level of enlightenment tries to teach this concept with only a superficial understanding, it is obvious that people will be led towards nihilism.

It may be true to say, "This body is not a Bodhi tree, the mind is not a clear mirror stand. Neither body nor mind essentially exists; there is essentially nothing [void and emptiness] so where will there be any dust or dirt?" [from the gatha in Tsu t'ang Chi, or Patriarch's Hall Collection]. However, this idea allows no possibility for discipline or development.

"Void and emptiness," is a similar idea to the Bodhidharma's words, "Vast Emptiness, Nothing Holy." In modern terms, this can be described as follows:

"The human body is nothing but a collection of molecules. Molecules are made up of atoms, which consist of protons, neutrons, and other particles. These can be further broken down into quarks. The invisible quark is set in motion by adding some heat energy—that is the human body.

"Humans are just collections of quarks that move around and bumping into each other, so how can concepts such as good or bad exist? I am a mass of quarks and so are you. We are just collections of these tiny particles moving around.

"People talk of the spirit body or spiritual energy, but it is doubtless some kind of kinetic energy. It must be the heat energy of the tiny particles of matter moving around. If the particles were to be separated, nothing would exist. So what is the point of such quarks in determining something is 'good or bad,' 'enlightened or not enlightened'?"

This is one way of looking at the world, and it is true that it presents a way of casting off attachments. At the same time, however, it will open another gate into nihilism.

## False logic in Zen Buddhism

The Zen of sudden enlightenment was started by Hui-neng, but we cannot necessarily say that this kind of enlightenment was unique to him. The philosophy of the founder of Zen, Bodhidharma himself, had many of the same features.

When Bodhidharma arrived in China from India, he met a man named Hui-k'o, who was later to become the second patriarch of Zen. There is one instance when Hui-k'o said to him, "My mind is anxious. Please pacify it."

Bodhidharma replied, "Bring out your wavering mind, and I will pacify it."

Hui-k'o said, "Although I've sought it, I cannot find it."

"There," Bodhidharma replied, "I have pacified your mind."

The record of this dialogue remains to this day. From this dialogue we can see that the subject of discussion has slightly changed. When Bodhidharma tells Hui-k'o to show him his mind, the word is metaphorically used as a material, physical object. He says, "Bring out your mind," to which Hui-k'o replies he cannot, then Bodhidharma says, "There, I have pacified your mind," meaning, "Your problems are solved." He meant that if Hui-k'o could not physically show him his mind, then it would be unable to retain any worry.

However, this is not a true form of enlightenment. Bodhidharma had changed the subject. If it had been Shakyamuni Buddha, he would have clearly put in words the mistaken ideas in Hui-k'o's mind. But Bodhidharma was not able to do this.

Zen Buddhism started from these roots so it would not necessarily be right to say that it was Hui-neng's problem alone. The enlightenment of Zen itself contains this sort of false logic to a considerable degree.

From Hui-neng's time, the use of obscure Zen dialogues has been prevalent. For example, when asked, "What was the significance of Bodhidharma having arrived from India?" the priest Chao-chou responded, "An oak tree in the garden" [according to *The Gateless Gate*, Case 37]. In another example, when asked the essential meaning of Buddhism, a certain priest would respond by raising one finger. Whenever he was asked a religious question he would always just raise one finger [the priest T'ien-lung and his disciple, Chu-chih, who appear in *The Gateless Gate*, Case 3, are well-known for this practice].

In this way, they rigidly insist that there are things that cannot be explained in words. However, while it is certainly true that there are things that cannot be explained verbally, it is a fact that Shakyamuni Buddha educated people by explaining enlightenment through his sermons. From this we can see that the ability to express things through words is definitely superior in terms of spreading the Truth.

While there are things that cannot be expressed in words, you should not interpret this inability as being unnecessary to express certain ideas in words. If you do, you are simply employing false logic and it is a low-level enlightenment.

## Hui-neng was the type of person
## Who made unexpected remarks

There is no doubt that the Southern sect of Zen was a new religious form of Zen in China at the time. Hui-neng was the legendary founder of the Southern sect of Zen, which has continued to the present day.

As the Southern sect was based on "sudden enlightenment" where each person would experience enlightenment in his own way and express it in a different form, it led to the formation of numerous branches. Different people would create a sect based on a different form of enlightenment in this way, and the creation of diverse groups indeed resulted in a lively atmosphere. It could be described as the democratization of Zen.

Hui-neng placed a strong emphasis on having insight into the true nature of things, and this would create the foundation for an increased interest in Zen in later years. This is one of his achievements.

However, looking at Hui-neng's character, he seemed very eccentric. Even today, there are people who act quite oddly but occasionally surprise everyone by saying something to the point. There are cases where someone with a rural background thought to be a simple person suddenly makes a shrewd comment that astonishes those around him. For instance, he or she may offer some penetrating insight into the character of a prime minister, which people realize is correct. Hui-neng must have been this sort of person.

At the time when the fifth patriarch Hung-jen was aged and thinking of retiring, Hui-neng had just come to live at the temple. Still in his early twenties, he had not yet started schooling for the priesthood nor had he qualified to be a monk. He had no education, he could not read or write, and had not studied the sutras [although it is believed that he had learned the Diamond Sutra, the Nirvana Sutra, the Lotus Sutra, the Vimalakirti Sutra and other sutras by listening to other students recite them]. Despite this, he made extremely astute comments and was chosen to be Hung-jen's successor. After Hung-jen read Hui-neng's gatha he was amazed and named Hui-neng as the next patriarch.

By rejecting Shen-hsiu, who had conventional knowledge and instead passing the mantle of leadership to Hui-neng, Hung-jen caused an uproar in the temple, which resulted in Zen being split into two sects, the Southern sect and the Northern sect. [Soon after the incident, Shen-hsiu also left Hung-jen's temple.]

There can be no doubt that Hui-neng was very gifted. Despite the fact that he was unable to read, he was highly perceptive and able to say things that would take everyone by surprise. However, people of his type often have a tendency to believe that just because they have that ability, everyone else should too.

For example, in the world of business, there are people who are successful without a prestigious academic background. Some people achieve success without even having finished elementary school. There are actually people like this and there is nothing wrong with it. It is, in fact, possible for someone to become successful without an education. However, if they were to insist that the reason they were successful was because they did not have an education, they would be wrong. If they really believe this, then it means that they are denying the effectiveness of any education. It would be the same as saying that there is no need to study. This would make it very difficult for them to carry out any kind of activity on a large scale.

People of this kind tend to run their businesses by following their intuition. As long as the business remains below a certain size, there will be no problem relying on their intuition, but once their company grows larger, intuition alone can no longer work. At that stage, it will become necessary for each department of the company to judge things based on rational thinking. Without it their business will not be able to expand. If everyone acts on his or her own as they come up with new ideas, it will create confusion in the company.

The same kind of problem occurred in Zen Buddhism, especially in the evolution of the Southern sect based on sudden enlightenment; the different branches all act in different ways and it has resulted in real confusion. But the very existence of variety in the teachings would appeal to a wider range of people, and that is why a number of odd characters have continually appeared in the course of history, resulting in the sect continuing to thrive.

## Shakyamuni Buddha's way of thinking Is not based on sudden enlightenment

If Hung-jen had really thought about making Hui-neng his successor, he should first have had him enter the priesthood formally, teach him how to read and write, and then have him study the sutras. And when Hui-neng had reached a certain level, then at that time he could have appointed him as his successor.

This was Shakyamuni Buddha's way. In the Lotus Sutra, there is the parable of the wealthy man and his impoverished son who had been missing for years. After having the son work as a lowly servant, then as head clerk for several decades, the rich man makes the son his heir. From this parable, it is evident that Shakyamuni Buddha supported such thinking. His teachings were not generally based on sudden enlightenment, although he did teach to his early disciples a simple form of enlightenment to be awakened as arhats. Basically, he expected his followers to devote themselves to spiritual discipline with continual perseverance.

However, since the robe and bowl had been passed down to an eccentric person with an extremely odd way of thinking, Zen Buddhism moved into ideology that promoted bizarre dialogues, disregarding logic and ethics.

In *The Platform Sutra of the Sixth Patriarch*, Hui-neng himself stated that he could not read or write, so he could not read any of the Sutras, but he could understand their meaning if they were read out loud. It may have been exaggeration or a way of humbling himself. This is the origin and background of the Zen sect that teaches sudden enlightenment, how it emerged from within the framework of Buddhism. [But it must be noted that in *The Platform Sutra of the Sixth Patriarch*, Hui-neng says in his own words, "Dharma is not essentially about sudden or gradual. Rather it is people who are sharp or dull." In this way he offers a critical view of the Northern sect's method of gradual enlightenment, suggesting that clever people can achieve sudden enlightenment, while slower thinking people can only achieve enlightenment gradually.]

# 4

# Work Ability and Enlightenment Are Interrelated

It is generally said that the more one studies and the more cultivated one becomes, the more pessimistic one is. This is because the more a person studies and the more knowledge he or she gains, the more that person realizes how prone humans are to making mistakes. They become more aware of how often humans make mistakes in real life and society, and understand how many people have destroyed themselves for the sake of greed. In this way people come to know the evil side of humans and that is why it is often said that the more educated people are, the more pessimistic they become.

On the contrary, uneducated people are often very quick to become conceited. This is frequently seen in the world of religion as well. For example, in the early days of Happy Science, when there were still not so many teachings and only a few books have been published, certain people would receive good scores, like ninety or even one hundred on their tests of teachings. This led them to believe that they were highly enlightened and they became conceited.

However, as new teachings are continuously given year after year, and as they increase in number and in depth, it naturally becomes harder and harder to absorb them all. Even if you once scored 100% on the Truth Exam, making you think that you are already enlightened, or that your enlightenment is greater than anyone else's, you will quickly start to regress in a year or two.

There is a tendency for people with insufficient worldly study and inexperienced in social perspective to quickly become conceited after a small success. On the other hand, those with a good understanding of the world are well aware that even though they have succeeded in achieving 100% on an exam, it does not necessarily mean that they are capable in the workplace as well.

Even if you have received a perfect score on a test after spending a month thoroughly studying a book and memorizing it all, you should not pride yourself as if you had conquered the world. While it may be true that you worked hard for the exam, if you take the same test again about a month later, you may not remember much of what you studied. Although cramming for a test in a short period of time may bring you some success, it is not a significant achievement.

Work ability and enlightenment are interrelated so you need to work continuously to refine your worldly skills as well. It is important that you also value worldly knowledge and experiences.

*Chapter Four*

# THE MOMENT OF GREAT ENLIGHTENMENT

*The Mystical Multi-Dimensional Space*
*Revealed by the Great Enlightenment*

# 1
## The Starting Point
## Of Enlightenment

More than twenty years have passed since I attained Great Enlightenment in March of 1981 [at the time of the lecture]. What was like a small spring in the beginning, welling up in the shadows of trees and rocks in the mountains, flowed to gradually become a stream, then a river, and then turned into a huge river, pouring into the ocean. I have seen this sight with my own eyes.

Over the last twenty years, the nature of my enlightenment has changed and evolved. At the same time, as I started to teach about enlightenment, my environment and organization have also changed. So here, I would like to return to the starting point and confirm what enlightenment is.

I would like to look back over the path that I have walked and consider the essential elements of enlightenment. I believe that doing this will help to verify whether what I have experienced is similar to or different from what is called "enlightenment" by the various religions of the world, and to what is believed to be the enlightenment of Shakyamuni Buddha [Gautama Siddhartha] in the stream of Buddhism.

Spiritual phenomena are, of course, a rare occurrence, but since there are many people who have testified that they have had such experiences in Japan and other countries, I cannot say they are uncommon. By examining how one's enlightenment has developed following a spiritual awakening, we can understand for the first time what was its root, the starting point of enlightenment, and tell whether the core elements of such an enlightenment were correct or not.

# 2

# The Philosophy of Egolessness

## Misunderstanding of the philosophy of egolessness

Examining the philosophy of Shakyamuni Buddha from various perspectives, the most famous, and at the same time the most confusing subject for scholars in Buddhist studies is the philosophy of egolessness.

In Indian philosophy, there is the word, *Atman*, which has multiple meanings, and among them are "soul" or "spirit," as well as "ego." And in Buddha's teachings, there is a record of him giving the teaching of *Anatman*, which has the opposite meaning of Atman. Although this teaching actually is used to show the enlightenment of Shakyamuni Buddha, it has also caused misunderstanding. He used the negative form of the word "Atman" to express his enlightenment and indeed it was significant to do so, but the use of that word has also been the root of a misunderstanding. So what is this philosophy of Anatman, or "egolessness"?

The concept of egolessness does not mean that self, in terms of one's recognition of oneself as a human being, does not exist, nor does it mean that humans are without souls. This is what I can definitely state from my personal experience.

There are some Buddhist scholars who have explained Anatman as the philosophy of no-soul. As Buddhism, and religion as a whole, have merely adhered to formality and been declining, they felt their status coming under threat and needed to infuse their philosophy with some kind of modern thinking. So they followed the ideas of post-Kantian philosophy, which separates spirituality from the philosophical self.

They also interpreted Buddhism in the light of communist ideas based on Marxist philosophy from over a hundred years ago. In this way they proclaimed that Buddhism had an up-to-date outlook, attempting to guarantee their own future. Advocating Buddhism like this, they probably thought that they had modernized it. Or perhaps in their youth they had become so engrossed in Marxism that they knew no other way to interpret Buddhism.

A philosophy has numerous facets and depending on which way you choose to look at it, it would appear quite different. The teachings of Shakyamuni Buddha, too, can appear to lead to materialism if you take only the philosophy of Anatman, the philosophy of non-ego, and interpret it as the denial of self or soul.

If you were to focus only on Buddha's teaching of the impermanence of all things, like in the statement, "Just as houses made of mud will be washed away when the River Ganges floods, so too will human physical bodies eventually perish," then it might also appear to be a worldly, materialistic thought. If you take this metaphor to mean simply that "all that has form in this world will eventually decay," then it is possible to claim that it is no different than materialism. However, this kind of interpretation arose because Buddha's enlightenment was far beyond the experience and understanding of those who tried to explain his philosophy.

## It is 100% true that spiritual beings exist

Religions exist all over the world, and even in the days when there were no sophisticated means of transportation or communication, there were many religions in different regions of the world that were founded on the same basis of the Truth. In every religion, there is a great being of Light corresponding to God or Buddha, and there are many teachings of life after death and reincarnation.

From these it would be evident that spiritual beings inhabit a world beyond this one, and that there also exists a being of great guiding Light. This view of the other world is the Truth that will last eternally as long as religion as a whole is not totally dismissed.

Among the elements of enlightenment I attained in 1981, the most essential point that cannot be ignored is the actual sensation that spiritual beings do exist. Of course I believed in spiritual things prior to that, and assumed that human beings were reincarnated repeatedly and that a Being known as God or Buddha existed. Still, it was a great shock to me to have been able to grasp its real meaning and confirm it as truth, rather than merely understanding it philosophically.

From both my experience and the enlightenment that Shakyamuni Buddha attained under the Bodhi tree more than 2500 years ago, I must conclude that enlightenment is not possible without spiritual awakening. In his reflective meditation that had continued for several weeks, Gautama Siddhartha [Shakyamuni Buddha] shed the shell of his ego and looked into his true self, thereby getting a brief view of the spiritual world that was confirmed real. This was not something that was achieved by chance; through his own contemplation and discernment he confirmed the existence of the spiritual world and was able to explore it. This actual experience must have given him an unshakable conviction.

## The mind is connected to the great universe

What, then, did Shakyamuni Buddha see after he removed the clouds covering his mind and went into deep meditation while sitting cross-legged under the Bodhi tree?

Shakyamuni Buddha actually saw a world different from this Earth with all its people moving about like tiny being. Rather he saw inside his mind where he was connected with a vast and boundless universe. He discovered that his inner universe was not confined to his physical body limited by a certain shape and size; instead, his being expanded boundlessly and was connected to an enormous universe, a universe that completely enveloped this three-dimensional world that we see.

He saw the mystical, limitless multi-dimensional space that the Primordial Buddha [Primordial God] of the great universe created. His own soul of course existed within this framework, but beyond it was a spiritual world, where "brother and sister souls" and other beings of Light resided [refer to Chapter Two of *The Laws of the Sun*]. There, the realms of heaven and hell also exist, where souls live in happiness or in unhappiness. Such a vast and boundless spiritual universe was connected to his internal self. This is what he discovered.

This is not to deny your existence. You are yourself, but at the same time you are not. While you exist in this world, you are not an independent being, cut off from everything else. You are not the kind of existential "ego" that modern philosophy and literature has been seeking to define.

Within your being is something that is connected to the great universe. By this, I do not mean the world limited by this small planet of third dimensional existence, but a much greater world that envelops more than that. Within you is a world that is connected to the great universe. Shakyamuni Buddha did not have to wait for the likes of Magellan to set sail in the Age of Discovery; he was able to travel freely to the furthest worlds by looking within.

## The enlightenment of "self and others are one"

Shakyamuni Buddha then awakened to the truth that the self and others appear to be discrete beings when viewed on the primary level of spiritual sight, but when examined more deeply, they are not separate but one. This means that although the self and others, or your soul and others' souls, may appear to be disconnected, this is not actually the case.

Of course your soul is connected to your brother and sister souls who have a close connection to you, but that is not all. Besides your brother and sister souls, there are other beings that exist in the vast and boundless spiritual world. There are human souls and also those belonging to other life forms, such as animals and plants. While they all appear to be distinct from each other, they actually cooperate and are interdependent. Shakyamuni Buddha awakened to this truth of the world.

In the same way that all the members of an orchestra play their individual instruments while simultaneously performing as a cohesive whole, all beings and life forms in the great universe work to produce the great music composed by Primordial Buddha [Primordial God]. Shakyamuni Buddha discovered that this was the sort of world in which people live.

## The Greater Self

What can we see if we apply this view of the world to the philosophy of egolessness?

When people live in this world, they think of themselves as their physical bodies, but there is more to a person than just their body. There is certainly the soul, which is exactly the same size and shape as the physical body, and although it too seems to be finite, it is actually something that is finite yet infinite; it is connected to the great universe.

In the world of the subconscious, the soul is connected to the vast and boundless spirit world, while also being connected to people's shared, common consciousness, or the world of spiritual thought energy that is common to all humanity. It acts like a telephone or a television, allowing instantaneous communication between all spiritual beings.

People may appear to live in separate bodies, but just like telephones, each person is connected to all others wirelessly. That is the way they are; each individual has his or her own "number," and everyone actually exists in linked contact with everyone else. What, then, joins everyone together? In truth it is the "laws of the mind."

The laws of the mind are universal, and they apply to all people, beyond race, sex, age, or even time. Some of the shared laws of the mind are, "If you possess a certain kind of mind, you will be attuned to that certain kind of world, you will be connected to persons of that type," "If you have certain kinds of thoughts, a certain kind of future will happen to you."

Shakyamuni Buddha looked into his inner self and realized that: "Spiritual beings are not separate selves, but are all connected to the eternal soul, to the eternal Greater Self. The minds of individual people are all connected to one another." To put it in modern terms, "There is more to you than just the superficial consciousness. There is also a subconsciousness that is connected to you, you are attuned to this subconsciousness as well." This subconsciousness is your own but, at the same time, it can connect instantaneously with all the different beings in the spirit world.

This is something which I also experience in my daily life. When I am watching TV, right away I am able to connect to the consciousness of the person on the screen. The same is true when I look at a photograph; I find myself able to connect with the consciousness of all kinds of people. Sometimes I even link to a person's guardian spirit, or to the lost spirits possessing that person. When I look at a photograph of a deceased person, sometimes the soul of that person comes and visits me. In this way, the other world is a world where everything connects in an instant. It is a world where a powerful network exists.

In fact, Shakyamuni Buddha was able to view the self that is connected to the spirit world, which differs from the readily seen physical self, and he expressed this as "egolessness." By "egolessness" he did not mean that the self does not exist, but that the self is connected to the enormous Greater Self. He meant, "Human beings are all connected to the Greater Self and they have a mutual influence on one another. They seem separate and yet they are not; they seem to be one and yet they are not."

Shakyamuni Buddha realized this was the kind of world we live in, and that the great will of Primordial Buddha [Primordial God], His will of self-actualization, has manifested as our individual lives, allowing us to bloom like flowers. The philosophy of egolessness can be explained in this way in the context of spatial awareness.

## Towards a philosophy of altruism

To put it another way, this philosophy of egolessness leads quite naturally to altruism. When we have awakened to the fact that we are not living alone, isolated from others, we will come to understand that an altruistic action means knowing and nurturing our original selves, and an altruistic heart means loving and cherishing the souls of contemporaries living in the same age as we do [refer to Chapter One and Two of *The Origin of Love* (New York: Lantern Books, 2003)].

Therefore, altruism and a love for others is also a form of egolessness. Once you realize that you are more than just your physical self isolated in this world, your mind will open up to altruism, and you will start to act based on it.

Shakyamuni Buddha's philosophy of egolessness teaches the importance of knowing the vast and boundless expanse that exists within one's own mind and of mastering the laws that govern it. At the same time it also teaches the meaning of human life: We are expected to view with compassionate eyes the many others who are undergoing soul training as we are, and to nurture and guide them on the path to mutual happiness. This is the enlightenment of egolessness. We must not neglect this point.

In the world of religion or among people with psychic ability, there are many who possess spiritual sense. But as long as they remain interested only in spiritual matters and do not develop a sense of altruism or love for others, their souls are destined to the Rear Heaven, where the Sennin [hermit] Realm and the Tengu [long-nosed goblin] Realm exist.

To join the soul group in the Front Heaven, where there are *bodhisattvas* [angels] and *tathagatas* [archangels], you need to know your true self, and knowing your true self must lead you to act for the benefit and love of others. This kind of enlightenment is required. Religions that encourage the achievement of this state are ones that have the power to develop society as well.

# 3

# The True Nature of Energy

## What genuine religions have taught

Enlightenment is vast and boundless, and there are various methods of teaching or explaining it, but the most important point to understand is that enlightenment is not possible if one disregards spiritual existence. Any thinking that denies the spiritual being is a mistaken modern interpretation of religion and Buddhism, which has been tainted by erroneous modern philosophy.

It is also essential to know that we are spiritual beings, and that we are connected to the vast spiritual universe, as well as to other spiritual beings. Heaven and hell are not only places that can be experienced externally, but also within our own minds. Our minds can move in any direction, and the needle of our minds can move omnidirectionally and so we can attune to any part of the spirit world. The needle of the mind, which is endowed in every human living in this world, has a mutual influence on one another. We need to know this.

Once we have this perspective of the universe, we will come to love others the same way that we love ourselves. The so-called golden rule, "Do unto others as you would have them do unto you" is drawn from this fact.

Seen in this way, the meanings of various religious teachings become clear. The first point is: "When souls who had assumed individuality in the distant past reside in a physical body, they tend to mistakenly believe that its current body is its true being, and consider themselves separate from others. As a result, they develop strong egos. Souls can make this mistake so there is need to correct them."

The second point is: "We must awaken to the fact that the physical being is not the true self. We must awaken to our spiritual selves, and understand that these spiritual selves are living as part of the harmony of the great universe, a world where people love and cherish each other." These are what the genuine religions of the world have taught.

If you lose this awareness and live a life with a self-deluded view based on the physical body, after death you will find that there will be nowhere for your spiritual being to go. It will remain wandering in this earthly world, possessing living people, or live in a dark place called hell where there is no light, believing it is still alive on Earth.

To save people from meeting this end, it is necessary to teach them the correct view of the world from the spiritual point of view, the right way to live, and the right view of life. We must then teach them that they should adjust their thoughts to this right way of living.

In his teachings, Shakyamuni Buddha talks of devils

and some people have interpreted this from a philosophical or psychological standpoint simply referring to them as delusions of the mind, but his words should be taken as real. Devils really do exist, as do Brahma and the gods. We must also know that anyone can become like these beings.

If you are living a hellish lifestyle, the inhabitants of hell will come to you. Just as angels try to increase their numbers, so do the spirits in hell, always looking out for people they can likely recruit. Since the vibrations of this earthly world are strongly materialistic, it is easier to be influenced by hell than by heaven. This is something we have to be aware of.

In order to change people's attitude and ways of thinking, religions have traditionally denounced material things and worldly lifestyles. First, they disapprove of their followers living in worldly lifestyles, by giving them strong admonishment against material desires. They advise, "You must not seek material possessions, you must not strive to obtain money. You must not pursue the opposite sex. You must not crave new clothes and you must not desire a new home," teaching their followers to give up various desires.

However, the important point is not the denial itself; the only reason they teach these things is to help people let go of their attachments to a worldly lifestyle. Once you have freed yourself of attachments and awakened spiritually, you will realize that there are many things in this world that serve to help improve people's lives, enrich them, and elevate their minds to a higher level.

"The denial of denial" is different from "simple approval." First you have to achieve the perspective of the spiritual self, then, look for more positive meaning in this world.

## The power of life and spiritual power
## Are opposite sides of the same power

There are many religious teachings that speak out against overindulgent desires for eating and drinking, sexual behavior, and sleep. They do this because the first step in achieving spiritual awareness is the denial of the powers of this world.

Nevertheless, if you turn your perspective and look at this from the opposite side, you will see that these earthly powers are those that enable life and also spiritual power. In fact, the power of life and spiritual power have much in common. They are reverse sides of the same power. If you lose the power to live in this world, you will also lose your spiritual strength.

For example, would it be considered acceptable to fast until one dies? Of course not. That is certainly not the way to turn this world into heaven. The power to live, to work, and to enrich others are also earthly powers.

The power to live comes from life energy, and life energy is obtained from food. Where then, does this food energy come from? Obviously it comes from the land, but that is not all. It ultimately comes from the sun's energy.

Receiving and absorbing light energy from the sun, the plants enrich the soil over a period of time so that new plants can grow to become energy sources for animals to eat and thrive. These animals too become food for other animals. Looked at in this way, it becomes clear that the power to live, life energy itself, has its origin in the energy of the sun.

## The law of substitution
## That works in this world and the spirit world

A sun, identical to the one we see in this world, also exists in the spirit world. It is what is known as the "spiritual sun." This spiritual sun has a slightly different color from the one we can see from Earth, being somewhat whiter. This spiritual sun sends out light energy to the other lives in the great universe.

The spiritual energy of the spiritual sun and the light energy of the sun of this world are actually opposite sides of the same energy. When it appears in this world, it takes on a material form whereas in the other world it does not, but the energy remains the same. This is the reason why things from this world and things from the spirit world are able to pass from one world to the other.

Recently, advanced physics has discovered the existence of elementary particles that can pop up into appearance, then suddenly disappear again. They come and go like ghosts and large numbers of these particles have been discovered. The fact is that these particles are fluctuating between spiritual energy and earthly energy. These elementary particles, the smallest bits of matter known to man, travel between the spirit world and this world.

The reason they are able to do this is that the energy of the spiritual sun and the energy of the sun in this world are opposite sides of one being. The energy that radiates from the spiritual sun becomes united with the light energy of the sun in this world and spreads through the great universe. The energy of the spiritual sun fills the beings living in the spirit world with its energy, while the light energy of this world's sun nurtures plants and animals on Earth. And these two forms of energy are combined through the process of reincarnation. Together forming opposite sides, separating into two, and rejoining as one, their energy travels around the great universe.

One of the laws of physics states that matter and energy are equivalent. It is understood that matter is merely a manifestation of energy and that it is possible to convert matter into energy. This is well-known as a law of physics, but the majority of people do not know the real meaning of this fact. It actually means: "The spirit world and this world can be transposed from one to the other. It is possible for one to interchange with the other, for the law of transposition to take place."

In fact, spiritual beings can appear in this world as beings of this world, and it is also possible for things of this world to transport into the spiritual world. This means that material objects can appear out of nowhere and exist as matter in this world. At the same time, things belonging to this world can disappear as if vaporized. Human beings exist within this kind of field of magnetic energy.

## Everything can be reconverted to spiritual energy

I have explained that Shakyamuni Buddha's philosophy of egolessness was not a theory of materialism. The physical body is an ephemeral thing, like a mud house that is washed away in a flood. This could be interpreted in materialistic terms by saying, "you must not become attached to such things." But in fact, everything that exists in this world is merely a manifestation of energy.

The true nature of energy is spiritual energy. When the vibrations of this spiritual energy become coarser, they manifest themselves in this world as matter. Be it a house or a human body, it will eventually decay, return to the earth, then finally be reduced to spiritual energy.

There are many creatures living on the Earth, and even after this planet finally disappears, the life energies that were alive in this world will continue to exist in the spirit world and will never disappear. This is another law, "the law of imperishable energy."

The life energies of people and animals alive on the planet today, as well as those who lived in the past, will never be lost, even if the planet ceases to exist. This is one of the reasons why the spirit world is so vast and boundless, and why it nurtures so many lives. The living beings of the past create a magnetic field of energy in the spirit world, from which are produced modern beings.

Everything is a manifestation of a fundamental, great Will. Therefore, any thinking that entirely separates the material from the spiritual is misunderstood. It is essential to know that the material and the spiritual will in the end be united and return to oneness.

I have stated that the philosophy of egolessness is not a materialistic theory but, in a certain context, the philosophy of egolessness can be applied to matter. Everything returns to light, everything returns to the energy of Buddha and God, and in this sense, the philosophy of egolessness can be said to have a materialistic aspect.

The spirit or soul that remains after you lose your earthly body is simply the light of Buddha and God, retaining a certain form. The soul and spirit are not, in essence, substantial existence, but deep within them only Light exists.

# 4

# The Mission of Religion

In this chapter I have talked about the nature of Great Enlightenment, in relation to Shakyamuni Buddha's enlightenment. Put simply, the message does not differ very much from that of various other religions of the world. The Truth is the simplest thing there is. It is not complicated, but very simple.

From your view, if you can see both this world and the other world, then you can consider it true. If you can see yourself as a spiritual being, then you can consider it true. And if you can feel that you are always able to connect with other spiritual beings, then you can consider it true.

If you are determined to accomplish your mission in this universe, this great masterpiece created by Buddha or God, you need to make efforts in the direction that serves to increase the brilliance of all creation. You must not waste your life on earth. If you see others living a wrong and wasted life, make an effort to help them change their life into a shining life. That is the mission of a person who has awakened.

It is the mission of religion, the work of religious organizations or religious communities, to increase the number of people who have awakened. For this fundamental mission to be fulfilled, there can be no limit or end to their activities. Their activities must be never-ending and should be unlimited by space as well. It is important that, with strong will, you make efforts and discipline yourself every day, and spread the Truth far and wide.

# Chapter Five

# ALWAYS WALK WITH BUDDHA

### *Study the Laws of the Mind and Put Them into Practice All Through Your Life*

# 1

# What Is Your True Self?

## The characteristics of the human mind

Some of you may have heard the expressions, "the power of the mind" or "the value of the mind," but I presume that most people do not fully understand what they actually mean.

Two thousand five hundred years ago, in his enlightenment Shakyamuni Buddha actually perceived the laws of the mind. Having awakened to these laws of the mind, the Buddha came to experience what would happen when he used them, and gained wisdom through these experiences.

The true nature of the laws of the mind can only be understood with greater involvement with the spiritual world, so people may have a little difficulty understanding them by words alone.

The truth is that while living on earth, the soul resides in a physical body and the true nature of being human is not the exterior, visible form, but the part inside that is unseen. When observed by someone with enlightened eyes, this true self outwardly appears to be a spiritual being with the same size and form as the physical body.

But while it can express itself in this way through its shape, it also exists according to a set of laws.

In other words, if the human mind chooses to take a given form, it will appear in that way but at the same time, if it intends to work in accordance to laws or functions, it can also work like that. These are the characteristics it possesses.

This can be explained using the metaphor of a powerful acid solution. If the acid is just put in a beaker, it will take the shape of the container, and there will be no other effect. However, if it was poured on a certain material, it would start to bubble and eat away at the material. In the same way, an alkaline solution can also create a chemical reaction. Although they may look just like water, under certain conditions some solutions can quickly start working to dissolve any material they come into contact with. There are also solutions that can suddenly harden when a chemical agent is added.

Alternatively, there are materials such as cornstarch. When cornstarch is dissolved in water then heated, strangely enough, it will gradually start to thicken in its form. But this is not its true form; if it is cooled, it will once more return to a state similar to the original liquid.

The true essence of a human is very similar to this. If one wishes to take a set shape, it is capable of doing so; on the other hand, if it wishes to be without shape and exist solely as qualities or a function, it can do that, too. While a soul resides in a human body, it takes a certain form, like the cornstarch solution that has been heated to create a substance, but when death finally comes and it leaves the physical body, it will return to its original state without a specific form.

## In the spirit world, you recognize yourself By the characteristics of your mind

When humans die and become a spirit body, at first they retain the same form that they possessed while they were alive on Earth. But after several years have passed, they understand that it is not their true form and begin to exist solely as a mind.

While the words "spirit body" and "soul" refer to a particular shape, the "mind" does not necessarily denote a set shape. The mind is the working of one's human consciousness, or one's mental function. After a certain period of time has passed upon returning to the spirit world, you will cease to think of yourself in terms of a shape; instead, you will come to understand that you are your mind, that you are a function of the mind.

You may now have a particular perception of yourself and define yourself in many ways. For example, you may think of yourself as a warm-hearted person, or quite rational, or someone easily excited but quick to cool down, or having a very meek personality. These kinds of definitions can well express the function of your mind.

If you were asked what kind of person you were, you could describe yourself in terms of the functions of your mind answering, "My mind has these characteristics." And these characteristics of your mind are a kind of "serial number" or barcode, to identify yourself in the spirit world. So, when you hear that there is a being that possesses certain characteristics or tendencies of mind, you will be able to point out, "That is Mr./Ms. X who lives in such-and-such a place." In this way the characteristics or tendencies of a person's mind will be his or her identity.

In the spirit world, you are free to change your form in any way you like, so it is impossible to identify someone by his or her appearance alone. This is the true state in the spirit world.

While alive in this world, you reside in the physical body engendered by your parents, consume earthly nourishment to live, and recognize yourself by your outward appearance. You define yourself by what you can sense through the functions of your sight, hearing, smell, taste, and touch, or by how other people look at you.

However, your true self can only be expressed through various adjectives, saying for example, "I am a calm, tolerant person," "I am extremely enthusiastic," "I am a highly intellectual person who admires knowledge," or "I take things at a slow pace." This is your true self and when you return to the spirit world, you will take the form that expresses this character, so you will need to change your self-recognition.

# 2

# What You Come to See Through Meditation

## A feeling of oneness with Buddha

In religion, great importance is placed on the practice of concentrating one's mind. This is true not only of Buddhism, but also of Christianity and Islam. In other religions, too, some kind of meditation is practiced.

Meditation means to set aside time to shut out all external stimuli as much as possible and concentrate on your inner self to look inside your mind. As you further deepen your meditation, you will become able to communicate with Buddha or God, and you will find that your "self" dissolves to become one with Buddha or God. You will reach a state where you will feel, "Buddha is my 'self'; my 'self' is Buddha."

In Japan, images of the Buddha are enshrined in Buddhist temples throughout the land. From the viewpoint of Judaism or Islam, this may be criticized as idolatry, but there is actually some meaning in enshrining the statue of Buddha.

If you enshrine a statue of Buddha as an object of worship and sit in front of it to meditate, you will have the experience of the statue of Buddha entering into you and you will enter into the statue of Buddha, thereby becoming one with it. This is what is referred to in esoteric Buddhism as "the Buddha entering the self; the self entering the Buddha." There is a state where the image of the Buddha enters you while you enter the image of the Buddha, and the two combine in complete harmony to become as one.

Basically it would be ideal to achieve this state without using a statue of Buddha, but before you reach that level you need to use an expedient means for you to be able to envision the image of Buddha in your mind. You need to train yourself to concentrate your mind, while sitting in front of a statue of Buddha, and meditate with your hands together or in some other posture.

As you create a vision of Buddha in your mind and gradually cast off the earthly, three-dimensional vibrations, you will come to experience being one with Buddha. This is the true purpose of chanting in Buddhism.

## The pure golden part of the human mind

While you are experiencing this unity with Buddha, you will realize that there are two kinds of "self" in what you thought was your identity. In the same way that you pan for gold from a streambed, you can distinguish the gold, the part that shines, apart from the "gravel" inside of yourself, the personality you have built up through the years in this lifetime.

The "gravel" part is, in most cases, the husk that has formed in the course of your life based on the physical senses, the way of life in which you have believed your physical body was your true self. In other words, it is the tendency to choose a life that is most comfortable for you as a physical being. Much of this gravel has built up, like barnacles sticking to the bottom of a ship. While you are meditating you need to sort the pure gold from the rest.

As you carry out this sorting process, you will gradually come to understand not only the relationship between yourself and Buddha, but also the relationship between yourself and all other living things in this world. In other words, there are billions of people on Earth, each living their own lives with their own likes and dislikes, and you will become able to see the golden part within each of them, the part that shines with a golden light.

It is very difficult for someone who is unable to distinguish the golden part in his own being to discover it in others. On the other hand, someone who has discovered the golden part within himself in meditation can look at others with the same eye and he will be able to perceive the golden part, the golden light that shines in others' minds, or in their characters.

Once you are capable of this, you will realize that the golden part within you is actually connected to that part inside others. Moreover, you will be able to see that this golden part connects you with Buddha, and everyone else in the world is also connected to Buddha in the same way.

You will come to recognize that there is equality for all people, which is different from "equality of outcomes" often seen in democratic societies, or equality in the sense that "everything must be treated as equal regardless." You will gradually be able to see the golden part within each person, and attain the wisdom to see others as equal in essence.

## The trace of having been created

Furthermore, if you focus your inner eye and carefully observe the world, you will be able to see clearly that plants and animals also possess similar golden parts, that they have minds as well.

In 12th–13th century Japan, there was a distinguished priest belonging to the Kegon sect of Buddhism named Myoe [1173 – 1232]. Apparently he was psychic. If you study the writings about his life, you will come across the following story:

One night, while sitting in meditation by the fireplace of the temple, looking as if he were fast asleep, he suddenly spoke out to one of his disciples. "The poor thing. It might be too late now, but there is a sparrow in a nest under the eaves of the bathroom that is about to be eaten by a snake. Hurry, take a light and drive the snake away." The disciple did not really believe him, but taking a lantern, he went to the back of the building and found that just as his master had said, there was a snake poised to attack a sparrow. In spite of the darkness, Myoe had been able to see what was happening in another place.

This ability is possible for those with spiritual disposition; they can actually see what is happening in other places. This is quite common. These people may be unable to perceive things as they experience the day-to-day rough vibrations of this world, but when they are in a state of meditation, they can see these things very clearly.

As you enter into deep meditation you will be connected to different worlds and become able to see all kinds of things. You will be able to understand the workings of the minds of animals as well as the thoughts and feelings of plants. A deep meditative state will allow you to be attuned to such things. You will also perceive the thinking or feelings of someone with whom you have some tie, no matter how far away that person may be. Through that connection, you will naturally be able to feel what the other person is actually thinking at the moment.

In my case, for instance, if I want to know the current thoughts of a president of a certain country, I am able to do so within the range allowed by the heavens. In much the same way that it is possible to access a computer and retrieve its information, I can gain access to what a particular person is thinking. If I focus too much on it, there may even be a problem with too much sensitive information coming in.

In this way, by going deep within yourself, you can find a way that leads to the infinite universe. And from this infinite universe, it connects to each and every person. This ultimately means that everything that has been granted life on this earth, including non-human existence, retains a trace of having been created. Whether they be humans, animals or plants, all bear a trace of creation.

What is a trace of creation? It is an intrinsic power that allows each living being to exist. Whether it be a dog, a cat or a human, male or female, all life carries within it a power that enables it to exist. This power can be referred to as "Buddha-nature." It manifests itself through the laws of the mind. The trace that all living beings have been created is that they are endowed with the laws of the mind and live according to them.

# 3

# The Freedom of the Mind

## The characteristics of someone
## Who has attained enlightenment

Tientai Chih-i [538 – 597 A.D.], who is said to have been one of the leading figures in the founding of Chinese Buddhism, taught that the human mind is capable of expressing numerous different states ["the mind can attune to three thousand worlds"].

When speaking of a person's character, we say, for example, "He is calm," "He is generous," "He is intellectual," "He is enthusiastic," and so on. There are many ways to describe a person's character and we choose the one that specifies one's distinctive character. But in fact, there is no characteristic that is entirely absent in one person while present in another. Even though each person has different tendencies and possesses different degrees of each characteristic, all possess a range of these same elements in their personality.

Someone may have a reputation of being meek, but this is not to say that he will never lose his temper. Even a meek person can become angry too if he is repeatedly provoked. On the other hand, someone who is known for a short temper will not be angry all the time; there will be occasions when he is calm and kind as well. In this way, the manifestation of characteristics can vary; some are strongly manifested while others are not.

There is the Buddhist teaching of "the Ten Worlds" [each of the ten realms of beings contains the other nine in itself] and it states that everyone possesses a function of mind that allows them to be attuned to various worlds, such as the world of Buddha, the world of Tathagata, the world of Bodhisattva and even the world of Hell [refer to Chapter Two of *The Laws of the Sun*]. All these possibilities lie in our hearts and we are given the freedom to choose which world we want to tune into.

Some people know that we have been given this freedom and are able to take hold of their own minds to control them completely. This is the trait of people who have attained enlightenment. It is important to be able to recognize your own state of mind, including what has caused it to be as it now is and what will happen in the future if you think in a certain way. Furthermore, it is important to recognize the effect and influence of your mind on others, on this world, and the spirit world, as well as on your own future and that of the world.

Having truly grasped the laws of the mind to acquire freedom of the mind is the first condition for becoming enlightened.

## Thought energy affects the world like a magnet

There are many descriptions of ways to achieve success in the books published by Happy Science. Success, development and prosperity are all elements of the universe that Buddha or God created; these elements are abundant in the universe and can be found everywhere.

If you form and emit the thought energy of prosperity continuously, it will act like a magnet and affect the world surrounding you. When you sprinkle iron filings on a piece of paper and hold a magnet near it, the iron filings will be attracted by the magnet and create beautiful ripples. In the same way, if a person emits "electromagnetic waves" in the direction of prosperity, elements of success will be tuned to those waves and start to gather around him or her. Many elements of success—ideas, business partners, and money—will be attracted to him or her by this power.

In this way, the function of the mind can be quite substantial. Depending on the kind of mind you choose to have, you will be able to transform yourself and once you have changed, you will have the same effect as a magnet and possess the power to create. This power of creation will change both your present and your future, and can even change the future of others. Not only will it change you and others, but also it will simultaneously change the world and influence the universe.

## The work of Buddha's disciples
## Is to teach the right direction

I teach people about what constitutes my enlightenment in a variety of ways, such as giving lectures and writing books. Each of these books on Buddha's Truth is like a powerful magnet, which changes the minds of people as millions of copies are spread throughout the world.

The people who are attracted to these magnets will themselves be changed into magnets. Magnets have the power to change other objects into magnets, as can be seen in the fact that a piece of iron, which has been in contact with a magnet for a length of time will become a magnet itself and attract other pieces of iron.

This is actually what missionary work is. Having enthusiasm to teach the laws of the mind is in itself a kind of magnet that will spread the laws of the mind, helping the people who learn and master them live true and happy lives in this world. Those who have experienced the feeling of happiness in this way will in turn become new magnets, spreading the laws of the mind further. This is the process of missionary work.

I am talking here about the method of achieving happiness, but the opposite also does exist. In this world there are also people who possess destructive thought energies. These people possess magnets with negative qualities and sometimes bring great unhappiness to large numbers of people.

In particular, when a person with extremely destructive thought energy holds a high post or stands in a position of leadership, such as a political or ideological leader, he or she will become a real "opposite-effect magnet" and bring destruction and disorder to everything. This kind of situation actually does happen in the world.

The work of these opposing magnets has continued for thousands and even tens of thousands of years. And it is the apostles of God, the Angels of Light, the tathagatas and the bodhisattvas, who fight against it, continuously showing people where the "North Star" or righteousness stands, teaching them the direction of true north.

If you compare the righteous and destructive by their powers alone, both appear powerful and sometimes it is difficult to tell which represents the Truth. However, north is clearly north, and teaching the right direction is the work of Buddha's disciples.

## "Precepts" that each person observes voluntarily And "rules" that govern communal life

You have the freedom of mind to choose the direction you wish to direct your thoughts. By focusing your mind in a good direction, you will be strongly concentrated on your goal and there will be an increased likelihood that your wishes come true.

For instance, if you focus your thoughts on prosperity, prosperity will arise, and if you focus them in the direction of wisdom, you will gain wisdom. If you concentrate your thoughts on spiritual training, it will manifest. So, focus your thoughts in a particular direction, and it will become manifest.

Therefore, it is important that each person has precepts, or internal rules of conduct that are appropriate for them individually, which determine what they should and should not do.

Buddhism has *sila*, or precepts that each person sets for themselves and decides to observe, unlike traffic rules that are externally imposed constraints. For instance, you might make a New Year's resolution that you will read one book of Buddha's Truth every month; it would be your own precept.

Having decided on this course of action, if you were to miss reading a book one month, then it means that you have broken that precept. But there would be no punishment for breaking a precept. Nevertheless, you will be filled with guilt and remorse for failing to observe it, saying, "This will never do, I must make myself stronger, I must train myself to do better." In this way, your soul training will advance.

When people hear the term "precept," they will often think that it represents a loss of freedom, but in fact, this is not the case. Each person decides precepts for himself in accordance with his own level of spiritual training.

In Shakyamuni Buddha's order, lay members were expected to adhere to the Five Precepts [not to take life, not to take what is not given, not to commit adultery, not to tell lies, and not to drink intoxicants], but this was not necessarily to say that they had to follow them all. At first, they would work on observing one of them, then if they were capable, two or three. If they were capable of observing all five, it would be much better, and if they felt they could keep even more, then they could set themselves as many as a hundred or two. So, precepts are rules that people set for themselves and try to observe voluntarily, with the aim of improving themselves.

On the other hand, there are *vinaya*, or rules that do have penalties if violated. These are a set of rules created for the priesthood to allow them to live together in a community. Even today, boarding schools have many rules that must be adhered to. They stipulate what time the students must get up in the morning, what time they eat, what time the gates are closed, what time the lights are turned off, and so on; if a student does not obey them, he or she may be expelled. The vinaya are similar in that they also carry a punishment for disobedience.

In order for priests to harmoniously live in communal life, it was necessary to create rules to prevent them from interfering with each other's spiritual training. So they set up shared rules, which allowed them to enjoy freedom without infringing one another's rights and interests.

These were called vinaya, which were designed to preserve freedom as long as everyone would abide by rules, and thus made communal life possible. There were various punishments for those who broke the rules, depending on the severity of the case. For instance they might be ordered to undergo a week of self-reflection, or in extreme cases, be expelled from the group of followers.

In this way there are both precepts and rules in Buddhism; the precepts were adopted by individual free will, while rules were put in place to preserve communal life and there were punishments for those who did not adhere to them. While the priesthood was bound by the rules, lay people were not. The lay congregation only had certain precepts to follow, and violation of these precepts was not subjected to any punishment. The precepts were followed voluntarily, and the people were told, "Please make an effort to observe them. If you fail to observe them, reflect on the cause of the failure and try once again."

As long as the precepts were in accordance with the spirit of Buddhism, it did not matter what they were and people were free to create their own. In modern times some examples could be: "doing some exercise every day," "not overeating," or "not sleeping too much." In this way, the precepts of Buddha's time were obeyed out of free will and there was no punishment for those who broke them. That was how the Buddha's order worked.

While the term "freedom" can of course include self-indulgence, where you do anything you want, it also means self-control. There is a freedom associated with will power, the will to determine the purpose and the direction you wish to move in, to impose certain rules on yourself and live within the range of these rules. This freedom comes with responsibility; it is freedom with a sense of commitment. This concept of freedom that is backed by a sense of responsibility is the true essence of Buddhism.

Buddhism adopted an approach in which one strives to master the laws of the mind through spiritual training without disturbing others, and to access the deepest part of one's mind that are connected to the universe.

## Buddhism has free and tolerant teachings

The two main characteristics of Buddhism are "freedom" and "peace." Buddhism is an extremely liberal religion, it is not restrictive and this is reflected in its teachings as well.

In the twenty-five hundred years that have passed since the Buddha passed away, there have been a vast number of offshoots, different sects, each interpreting his teachings in their own way. Some of them even teach things that are in complete opposition to the Buddha's original teachings. Still, Buddhism is tolerant enough to allow this. In many instances people would take one part of Buddha's teachings and proclaim it to be the only Truth, but from the outset Buddhism demonstrated tolerance to accept them.

In Japan, for example, during the thirteenth century, a monk named Dogen [1200 – 1253] preached that Zen was the only true form of Buddhism. However, although it is indeed true that Shakyamuni Buddha practiced Zen meditation, it is not the whole of Buddhism; there are also the teachings of the mind and numerous other teachings.

There were also monks who claimed that the true essence of Buddhism was to be found in chanting the name of the Buddha. The most famous of these were Honen [1133 – 1212] and Shinran [1173 – 1262] who taught their followers to chant the words, "I put my faith in Amitabha Buddha."

However, the original purpose of Buddhist chanting was different. The original idea was, as I explained in section two of this chapter, to visualize an image of Buddha in your heart and become one with Him, that you focus strongly on the Buddha to be united with Him. So it was not just about chanting the words, "I put my faith in Amitabha Buddha." Nevertheless, this idea cannot be discarded altogether as it is possible to become one with Him through the repetition of these words.

Another example is a group that arose in the lineage of the Nichiren sect of Buddhism. It claims that the Lotus Sutra is the only true teaching of the Buddha, making it the foundation for all their activities, and the doctrine used for the conversion of other people to their faith. This may seem extreme, but it was true that Buddha's order had an aspect that sternly rejected mistaken ideas.

In this sense, Buddhism has numerous aspects and has been very tolerant of the variety of interpretations. This is the reason why, in its history of over twenty-five hundred years, Buddhism has seen the appearance of numerous teachings and new founders of various sects. Buddhist teachings are like the great movement of the River Ganges, swallowing everything in its current. There are even some sects that have preached the opposite of Buddha, giving the impression that Buddhism even allows them to flow against the current.

# 4

# Peace of Mind

## The tranquility of mind that modern people seek

The other major characteristic of Buddhism is that it displays an extremely strong desire for peace. When I say peace in this context, I am referring to peace of mind. Buddhism places the greatest value on peace of mind.

In three-dimensional worldly terms or contemporary terms, when you are able to say, "I achieved a great result by doing this activity," or "By doing this action, I was able to get a reward," you may often feel a sense of success, achievement, or happiness. However, that is not all there is to happiness.

Happiness in Buddhist terms is the extreme sense of quiet. It is found in a very tranquil and serene state, like the smooth surface of a mountain lake. When your mind is quiet and calm, as mirror-like still water without a single ripple, you will feel happiness. This is an essential point.

The value of this state of mind may seem to be the exact opposite of the values held by busy people in today's society, but we all share an instinctive desire for this quiet state. Even though people are extremely busy working, most of them are seeking an oasis, trying to get a moment of peace, but are unable to attain it. As a result, some people look to religion for their oasis of the mind, others seek it in academic life, while still others enjoy being with nature.

Modern people have an instinctive understanding of the value of enjoying a peaceful state, namely, peace and calmness of mind. However, they have yet to fully grasp the greatness of its value.


## What constitute the ground of the spirit world

Peace of mind is something that has very profound value. The spirit world is comprised of various levels—from the fourth dimension through the fifth, sixth, seventh and eighth to the ninth—each of these dimensions being further broken down into different realms [refer to Chapter One of *The Laws of the Sun*]. The boundary, or ground, which separates each of these different dimensions is actually one's peace of mind.

The dimensions are separated from one another according to the degree of peace of mind that their inhabitants have. A peaceful mind can be described another way as being an unwavering mind or an unshakable mind. Dimensional levels are formed according to the constant wavelengths or vibrations of the residents' minds.

This means that even though a spirit may currently reside in the seventh dimension, if the spirit's mind begins to waver with larger emotional fluctuations, and if that spirit's mind tends to become closer to that of a demon in hell, then the ground beneath it will suddenly split open, plunging the spirit to a lower level. It is just like descending in an elevator; the fall will be rapid and the spirit will no longer be able to live in the realm in which it used to reside.

In this way, the ability to sustain peace of mind is what creates the separation of the dimensions. Therefore, unless you have the ability to maintain your peace of mind at a certain level, you cannot stay in the realm where you used to reside.

The lower the realm which one descends, the more turbulent thought energies are and the more disturbed the vibrations of the mind. The fourth dimension is situated extremely close to the third dimension and its vibrations very closely resemble those of the world on Earth. Many of those who reside in the fourth dimension lead lives very similar to the ones they led on Earth, despite the fact that they do not possess physical bodies.

Furthermore, nearly all the inhabitants of hell are strongly drawn to earthly values. They cannot rid themselves of their attachments to the surface of the world on Earth and are unable to get free. They feel that they are unable to live without the constant pull of the "gravity" of earthly desire.

As a result, many of the spirits in hell come to possess people on Earth, and lead their lives sharing the same hobbies and diversions as living people. The fact that spirits are able to possess people on Earth and live with them for five, ten or even twenty years shows that both the possessor and the possessed share exactly the same views and values. There are many who live in this way.

Those in hell live in a completely opposite way to those who emit refined, steady, and peaceful vibrations. In the realm of hell, there are many who are highly volatile and have extremely destructive and rough thought energy.

## How to regain your peace of mind

Life in contemporary society is really busy so it is important that you regain your peace of mind while you are living in this society. There are several ways to achieve this.

One is to sit quietly on your own and read a book on Buddha's Truth. Another is to face your inner self by concentrating your mind or practicing meditation. Yet another is to practice self-reflection, removing the thorns that have pierced your heart one by one, carefully wiping away pitch-black stains from your mind as if bleaching spilled black ink.

If you are unable to maintain peace of mind by your own efforts, if you are in a state where you cannot possibly practice self-reflection or meditation, then all you can do is to resort to prayer. This is particularly true when you are being possessed by a malicious spirit, which is a powerful evil spirit, or if you have become deluded by a demon. In such cases, it is extremely hard to regain your peace of mind.

This is when your mind is constantly agitated and you are unable to organize your thoughts. Your mind keeps returning to the same thoughts over and over again; no matter how hard you try to change, you are unable to do so. You cannot free yourself of this attachment no matter how hard you may try. Moreover, thoughts that are opposite type of those you usually have relentlessly appear in your mind and turn your way of thinking around.

Unfortunately, when you are possessed by a powerful demon in this way, you are in no condition to practice self-reflection or meditation. All you can do at such times is to rely on strong prayers. So please pray to the guiding spirit group of Happy Science.

Pray, and help will come. This is guaranteed. If you are a Happy Science believer, pray to me by reciting "Prayer to the Lord" or "Prayer to El Cantare." One of the spirits from the Happy Science spirit group will certainly come to your aid and imbue your heart with light. There are times when you cannot help but rely on prayer in this way.

## Even when busy, keep your mind as clear
## As the calm surface of a lake

It is essential to calm your mind and make it peaceful through self-reflection, meditation and prayer. The longer you are able to maintain a peaceful mind in this life, the higher the realm you will be able to inhabit after you return to the other world.

You may imagine that the inhabitants of the higher realms do not do any work, but that is not the case. They are actually extremely busy working on various missions. Among Buddhist statues, there are Eleven-headed Kannon [avalokiteshvara, or goddess] and Thousand-armed Kannon. These figures express the myriad of tasks that spirits in the higher dimensions attend to. They are helping many people all over the world and so are extremely busy.

However, no matter how busy they may be, they must not allow their hearts to become agitated or unstable. While working at a high level and across a wide range of areas, they must keep their minds calm and clear. These are the duties assigned to the spirits of the higher dimensions.

In the same way that success can be divided into shallow or genuine, people who work hard at their jobs can also be categorized into two groups: those who work in hellish ways and those who work in heavenly ways, like the Thousand-armed Kannon. Even when you have a lot of work and are busy working, you must always maintain a peaceful and clear mind that is like the surface of a mountain lake. This is true both in this world and the next. First, you need to begin by calming your own mind.

The calm, meditative mind is not something that can only be attained in a special environment. Once you have learned to maintain a constant peaceful mind, no matter what you are doing—whether you are walking, working or even talking on the telephone—you can maintain a meditative state. This is what is meant by "working as meditating." In this state, you are doing your job while continuing your spiritual training and calming your mind, and at the same time, looking deeply into the relationships between yourself and others, between you and the world, the relationships that span the entire universe.

Meditation is not only about sitting in a cross-legged pose. A meditative mind should dictate your life throughout the day.

## Entering nirvana while you are still alive

In addition to having freedom of the mind, it is essential to know the importance of having peace of mind. Buddhism seeks both freedom and peace of mind.

In Buddhist terms, the state of having a peaceful

mind is referred to as "nirvana." The higher realms of the world after death, are also known as the nirvana realms [or nirvana without remainder] and it is where tathagatas and bodhisattvas live in peace. It is possible to attain this peaceful state while still living on earth and it also is called "nirvana." This is called "liberation while alive." One can enter into the peaceful state of nirvana while still living in a physical body [nirvana with remainder].

The term "nirvana" means the state in which the "flames" have been blown out, the flames symbolizing "worldly delusions," or mental functions which disturb the mind. The mental functions which disturb the mind can be likened to discordant music. It is hard to continue listening to cacophonous music for a long time and, in the same way, it is hard to remain with an extremely disturbed mind. The state in which the flames of these worldly delusions has been extinguished, the state in which great serenity has been achieved, is the state of nirvana, and the purpose of meditation is to seek this state.

When you enter into deep meditation, worldly disturbances cease and you become one with Buddha and God. If I were to describe this phenomena, first your mind is filled with great peace, then you feel a warm light coming into your body. This feeling grows until you not only feel a warm light, but are actually able to see it shining. It then appears like a ball of light. Light appears and it becomes one with you. You will come to understand this sensation very clearly.

The gold-colored statues of Buddha are an expression of this state. When you are meditating, you will experience the sensation of being one with Light, and when you achieve this state, it can be said that you have nearly established a true state of nirvana.

According to Buddhist doctrine, once you have succeeded in creating this state in your mind while still living on Earth, you will be able to attune yourself to higher dimensional realms. If, for example, you are able to attain the state of mind that is attuned to the seventh dimension while still living on earth, you will be able to travel to and from it at will. It is possible for those in that realm to visit you, and also for you to travel there. From this circumstance it will be determined that you will go back to that realm after death. When you die, you will return to the realm that corresponds to your current state of mind. This is Buddhist doctrine.

I have been able to confirm this to be true through my long years of experience. These beings whose minds share the same state as yours will always attune themselves to you. The world that you are constantly attuned to is the one where you will go after you leave your physical body and become the mind itself.

But even if you might try hard to emit wavelengths that are attuned to the higher realms, it is usually not possible. In musical terms, for instance, if an ordinary person were asked to perform like the greatest world's violinist or pianist, he would find it impossible to do.

It may be possible for a talented musician to play like a bad one, but if a bad musician were asked to play like a talented one, he or she would be unable to do so. There is a highest possible level that each person is able to perform and this level depends on their talent and ability. The more they practice, the more they can continually give their best. The same can be said of the vibrations of the mind. This is what we need to seek to be in the state of nirvana.

# 5
## Missionary Work Means Spreading Wisdom

As I have explained here, the two characteristics of Buddhism are freedom and peace, both of which are to be found in enlightenment. Enlightenment that incorporates freedom and peace is called "wisdom." This "wisdom" does not belong to the individual; true wisdom is universal, it is something precious shared by the whole of humanity, and it is open to all.

Buddha did not attempt to keep his enlightenment to himself; he tried to share wisdom, the fruits of his enlightenment, with others. He taught others about the wisdom he had acquired, saying, "If you do this, you will be able to achieve enlightenment. If you discipline yourself, you too can be one with Buddha and God. So, aim to attain such a state." And he called the act of spreading this wisdom "missionary work."

The act of spreading wisdom is also the act of removing pain and sorrow from the minds of many people and so it is a form of compassion. It is also the practice of love. Missionary work is based on compassion and love; at the same time, it is love that turns into action. This is an important aspect of missionary work.

Buddha did not try to keep wisdom to himself but to share it with others as the common inheritance of humankind, a communal treasure for all. This intention turned into enthusiasm for his missionary work.

The Truth must be understood by as many people as possible, because it will bring happiness to many. It is shameful not to share with others the way to happiness when you know it. Someone who does not know the Truth can be likened to a person who walks a long distance to use the public baths every day, not knowing that a natural hot spring lies dormant under his own patch of land. Many people actually find themselves in such a situation. Missionary work is to tell them about the hot spring on their own garden plots, and teach them how to uncover it.

I have explained the relationship between wisdom and compassion. What is referred to in religions as missionary work, education, or spreading the teachings, means to spread wisdom. This is the work of Buddha's disciples.

# 6
## The Law of Cause and Effect

### The cycle of cause and effect
### Never fails to complete itself

Enlightenment in Buddhism also includes the law of cause and effect. Of the two elements freedom and peace, the law of cause and effect is more closely related to freedom.

There are two types of the law of cause and effect. One is "time causality," which is represented by a vertical line of time. In the flow of cause and effect, or in the chains of causality through past, present and future, humans live, society moves on, and history goes on.

Depending on what you do today, your life will change and so will the lives of those around you. As a result, the world will also change to some extent. If you are in a position of influence, your decisions can affect the direction of your entire company, society, the country or even the world. In this way, the future is a result of the accumulation of choices so it is essential to be deeply aware of the importance of your choices.

Buddha granted humankind freedom of mind and the law of cause and effect. Freedom of mind is always accompanied by responsibility. It means that we have to accept whatever happens as the consequence of our original action. It is something we have to be prepared to accept.

While the result of a particular action can manifest in this world, sometimes the cycle of cause and effect is not completed here. In that case, it will be completed without fail in the world beyond this one.

In this world, there may be times when you feel that you have not been rewarded in spite of all your efforts, while at the same time others may achieve great success with hardly any effort. If you only look at such outcomes by themselves, it may certainly seem unfair and that cause and effect does not necessarily seem to work. However, it is precisely because the cycle of cause and effect is not complete in this world that the following is the logical deduction: "The cycle of cause and effect will certainly be completed in the Real World that transcends this one."

In this world, it sometimes happens that good people die unhappy deaths. But they are not unhappy events in the truest sense; these people are guaranteed their reward in heaven. In this world on Earth, it may sometimes appear that evil people prosper, but their prosperity does not continue forever. It is sure to be a major attachment for them and will cause them suffering in the next world.

As you can see from this, good causes do not necessarily yield good results, and bad causes do not always yield bad results in this world; in fact it sometimes appears as if the opposite is true. In Buddhist terms, this is called *vipaka*, and its result *vipaka-phala*, or an effect which has a different moral nature from its cause.

This kind of phenomenon can be seen in a variety of situations. When it occurs, it simply means that the cycle of cause and effect has yet to be completed in this world but will be completed once the person has moved on to the next world.

What I have explained so far is the situation concerning the end of a person's life, but a similar situation can hold true at the beginning of one's life. Although we say that all people are children of Buddha and God and therefore all people are equal, there are actually differences in the circumstances of our birth. Some are born into wealth while others into poverty. There are yet others who were born with some kind of physical handicap, illness or disability. There are also differences in intelligence and physical strength; everyone is different and people are not necessarily equal.

When seen from the perspective of the present time, it may appear that these circumstances represent inequality and unfairness. However, you have to remember that the outcomes of past reincarnations continue to take effect. As for matters that are incomprehensible or inexplicable when you only observe this current life, you can assume that the original cause lies in your actions of previous lives.

It is only after taking this into account that you are

able to explain the differences which occur at birth. If this was not the case, everyone would be born the same. In reality, however, the only matter that is equal is the fact that all are born infants; there are differences in the gifts, abilities, constitutions, and other qualities they possess. It is because factors not only from this life are at work here.

The moment of birth is a beginning, but simultaneously, it is also a result. The result of a person's various journeys in past lives determines the starting point in this lifetime. The law of cause and effect does not finish a cycle in a single lifetime; it continues from the limitless past into the limitless future. This is the law of cause and effect through the progression of time.

## People live by mutual support

The law of cause and effect also has a spatial aspect. We support each other as we live and we live in a space where there is mutual support. There is support for each other between husband and wife, parent and child, among friends or even colleagues. This is what is known as interdependence. It is important to realize that people live out their lives depending on one another.

This can be likened to how trade impacts Japan and the United States. If Japan can supply goods at low cost to the United States, not only will the Japanese make some profit, but the Americans will benefit, too. Each country is connected and has an impact on others, and in this way the entire world develops and prospers.

The kind of causality that exists in commerce can also be found in interpersonal relationships. Living in this world means that people share mutual relationships in the space of this world, in other words, they live amidst a "space causality." Moreover, the fact that people live with mutual support means that the principle of love is at work within this world.

While humans must live responsibly in the flow of time, in the vertical chains of cause and effect, they also support each other in the horizontal sense of space. This understanding leads us to volunteer missionary work as acts of compassion, which I mentioned earlier. We must save many people because we can create a better age and society by supporting one another. Therefore, even from the viewpoint of space causality, missionary work is extremely important.

Missionary work will, of course, bring happiness to the person to whom you are conveying the Truth. But not only that, it will also make the world in which you live a better place, while at the same time it will nourish you. By improving yourself, you will improve others as well, and make the world you live in an even better place. In this way, it creates a cycle of goodness, which will also make the future better.

In fact, space causality means that we are living in a world where things influence one another endlessly. The world is like a fishing net that is comprised of vertical and horizontal lines, which have been knotted together. Each of the knots where the lines cross represents a person's individuality, with its own name and character. Each knot is separate, but only when the vertical and horizontal lines join together to become a net can the task of "catching fish" be accomplished.

In the same way, humans carry out a grand mission as we live together in community. As a single knot, they can achieve nothing. This net of interwoven lines stretches out to encompass the entire universe and is known as Indra's net. Everyone is a part of this vast net, independent in one aspect and at the same time connected to everyone else.

This net is formed by the Truth of the great universe, by the Will of Buddha of the great universe. People are part of a whole; they are a part, as well as a whole. They are alone but not alone; they are a huge multitude and yet individuals. This is the truth of life.

# 7

# Strive to Master the Laws of the Mind

I have spoken on the themes of "freedom and peace," "wisdom and compassion," and "the law of cause and effect," centered on the laws of the mind. In fact, all of these represent the Buddha's enlightenment. I have described Buddha's enlightenment in modern terms.

Strive to master the laws of the mind all through your life; study them and put them into practice while you are living. This is what is meant by "walking with Buddha."

Buddha walked the same road in the past and is still walking it now. As long as you strive to master the laws of the mind, you are walking with Buddha, as one of His disciples. To always walk with Buddha means to always examine your own mind, refine it and try to live in accordance with the laws of the mind.

I pray that this last chapter will serve to motivate you in your missionary work.

# Afterword

In Chapter One, I began with the story of Angulimala, first labeled a demoniacal murderer but later experiencing conversion, salvation and enlightenment. This was to express my determination to save all people through the divine power of Buddha.

In Chapter Two, I showed how I have incorporated the teaching of the power to forgive sins into the Laws I teach, just as Christ did historically.

In Chapter Three, I took a close look at the essence of Zen in relation to enlightenment. It is probably the first time in one thousand three hundred years that Hui-neng, who was at the start of the sudden enlightenment of Zen, has been criticized to this extent.

In Chapter Four, I covered the topic of my own enlightenment in this lifetime.

And in Chapter Five, I have demonstrated my strong resolve as a Buddha.

Only one Buddha is born in one age. You are now living in the age of a miracle. This being so, have courage and be confident. As long as you have faith, I am always with you.

*Ryuho Okawa*
*Founder and CEO of Happy Science Group*
*December 2002*

*This book is a compilation of the lectures
as listed below.*

- Chapter One -
## The Enemy Is Within You
Released on October 5, 1996

- Chapter Two -
## The Power to Forgive Sins
Released on January 7, 2001

- Chapter Three -
## Work Ability and Enlightenment
Released on November 23, 1997

- Chapter Four -
# The Moment of Great Enlightenment
Released on July 7, 2002

- Chapter Five -
# Always Walk with Buddha
Released on October 4, 1998

# ABOUT THE AUTHOR

Ryuho Okawa was born on July 7th 1956, in Tokushima, Japan. After graduating from the University of Tokyo with a law degree, he joined a Tokyo-based trading house. While working at its New York headquarters, he studied international finance at the Graduate Center of the City University of New York. In 1981, he attained Great Enlightenment and became aware that he is El Cantare with a mission to bring salvation to all of humankind. In 1986 he established Happy Science. It now has members in over 100 countries across the world, with more than 700 local branches and temples as well as 10,000 missionary houses around the world. The total number of lectures has exceeded 2,900 (of more than 130 are in English) and over 2,500 books (of more than 500 are Spiritual Interview Series) have been published, many of which are translated into 31 languages. Many of the books, including *The Laws of the Sun* have become best seller or million seller.

Up to date, Happy Science has produced 18 movies. These projects were all planned by the executive producer, Ryuho Okawa. Recent movie titles are *Life is Beautiful – Heart to Heart 2 –* (documentary released Aug. 2019), *Immortal Hero* (live-action movie to be released Oct. 2019), and *Shinrei Kissa EXTRA no Himitsu – The Real Exorcist –* (literally, "The Secret of Spirits' Café EXTRA – The Real Exorcist –," live-action movie to be released in 2020). He has also composed the lyrics and music of over 100 songs, such as theme songs and featured songs of movies. Moreover, he is the Founder of Happy Science University and Happy Science Academy (Junior and Senior High School), Founder and President of the Happiness Realization Party, Founder and Honorary Headmaster of Happy Science Institute of Government and Management, Founder of IRH Press Co., Ltd., and the Chairperson of New Star Production Co., Ltd. and ARI Production Co., Ltd.

# WHAT IS EL CANTARE?

El Cantare means "the Light of the Earth," and is the Supreme God of the Earth who has been guiding humankind since the beginning of Genesis. He is whom Jesus called Father, and His branch spirits, such as Shakyamuni Buddha and Hermes, have descended to Earth many times and helped to flourish many civilizations. To unite various religions and to integrate various fields of study in order to build a new civilization on Earth, a part of the core consciousness has descended to Earth as Master Ryuho Okawa.

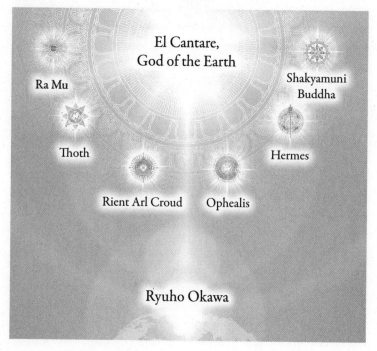

El Cantare,
God of the Earth

Ra Mu

Shakyamuni
Buddha

Thoth

Hermes

Rient Arl Croud     Ophealis

Ryuho Okawa

## Shakyamuni Buddha

Gautama Siddhartha was born as a prince into the Shakya Clan in India around 2,600 years ago. When he was 29 years old, he renounced the world and sought enlightenment. He later attained Great Enlightenment and founded Buddhism.

## Hermes

In the Greek mythology, Hermes is thought of as one of the 12 Olympian gods, but the spiritual Truth is that he taught the teachings of love and progress around 4,300 years ago that became the origin of the rise of the Western civilization. He is a hero that truly existed.

## Ophealis

Ophealis was born in Greece around 6,500 years ago and was the leader who took an expedition to as far as Egypt. He is the God of miracles, prosperity, and arts, and is known as Osiris in the Egyptian mythology.

## Rient Arl Croud

Rient Arl Croud was born as a king of the ancient Incan Empire around 7,000 years ago and taught about the mysteries of the mind. In the heavenly world, he is responsible for the interactions that take place between various planets.

## Thoth

Thoth was an almighty leader who built the golden age of the Atlantic civilization around 12,000 years ago. In the Egyptian mythology, he is known as god Thoth.

## Ra Mu

Ra Mu was a leader who built the golden age of the civilization of Mu around 17,000 years ago. As a religious leader and a politician, he ruled by uniting religion and politics.

# ABOUT HAPPY SCIENCE

Happy Science is a global movement that empowers individuals to find purpose and spiritual happiness and to share that happiness with their families, societies, and the world. With more than twelve million members around the world, Happy Science aims to increase awareness of spiritual truths and expand our capacity for love, compassion, and joy so that together we can create the kind of world we all wish to live in.

Activities at Happy Science are based on the Principles of Happiness (Love, Wisdom, Self-Reflection, and Progress). These principles embrace worldwide philosophies and beliefs, transcending boundaries of culture and religions.

**Love** teaches us to give ourselves freely without expecting anything in return; it encompasses giving, nurturing, and forgiving.

**Wisdom** leads us to the insights of spiritual truths, and opens us to the true meaning of life and the will of God (the universe, the highest power, Buddha).

**Self-Reflection** brings a mindful, nonjudgmental lens to our thoughts and actions to help us find our truest selves—the essence of our souls—and deepen our connection to the highest power. It helps us attain a clean and peaceful mind and leads us to the right life path.

**Progress** emphasizes the positive, dynamic aspects of our spiritual growth—actions we can take to manifest and spread happiness around the world. It's a path that not only expands our soul growth, but also furthers the collective potential of the world we live in.

## PROGRAMS AND EVENTS

The doors of Happy Science are open to all. We offer a variety of programs and events, including self-exploration and self-growth programs, spiritual seminars, meditation and contemplation sessions, study groups, and book events.

Our programs are designed to:
* Deepen your understanding of your purpose and meaning in life
* Improve your relationships and increase your capacity to love unconditionally
* Attain peace of mind, decrease anxiety and stress, and feel positive
* Gain deeper insights and a broader perspective on the world
* Learn how to overcome life's challenges
  ... and much more.

*For more information, visit **happy-science.org**.*

## INTERNATIONAL SEMINARS

Each year, friends from all over the world join our international seminars, held at our faith centers in Japan. Different programs are offered each year and cover a wide variety of topics, including improving relationships, practicing the Eightfold Path to enlightenment, and loving yourself, to name just a few.

## HAPPY SCIENCE MONTHLY

Happy Science regularly publishes various magazines for readers around the world. The Happy Science Monthly, which now spans over 300 issues, contains Master Okawa's latest lectures, words of wisdom, stories of remarkable life-changing experiences, world news, and much more to guide members and their friends to a happier life. This is available in many other languages, including Portuguese, Spanish, French, German, Chinese, and Korean. Happy Science Basics, on the other hand, is a 'theme-based' booklet made in an easy-to-read style for those new to Happy Science, which is also ideal to give to friends and family. You can pick up the latest issues from Happy Science, subscribe to have them delivered (see our contacts page) or view them online.*

*Online editions of the *Happy Science Monthly* and *Happy Science Basics* can be viewed at:
**info.happy-science.org/category/magazines/**

*For more information, visit www.happy-science.org*

## SOCIAL CONTRIBUTIONS

Happy Science tackles social issues such as suicide and bullying, and launches heartfelt, precise and prompt rescue operations after a major disaster.

### ◆ The HS Nelson Mandela Fund

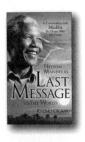

The Happy Science Group provides disaster relief and educational aid overseas via this Fund. We established it following the publication of *Nelson Mandela's Last Message to the World*, a spiritual message from the late Nelson Mandela, in 2013. The fund actively provides both material and spiritual aid to people overseas—support for victims of racial discrimination, poverty, political oppression, natural disasters, and more.

**Examples of how the fund has been used:**

Provided tents in rural Nepal

Supplied food and water immediately after the Nepal earthquake

Donated a container library to South African primary school, in collaboration with Nelson Mandela Foundation

♦ **We extend a helping hand around the world to aid in post-disaster reconstruction and education.**

<u>Nepal:</u> After the 2015 Nepal Earthquake, we promptly offered our local temple as a temporary evacuation center and utilized our global network to send water, food and tents. We will keep supporting their recovery via the HS Nelson Mandela Fund. In addition, we have collaborated with the Nepalese Ambassador in Japan to offer a portion of the profit from the movie, *The Rebirth of Buddha*, to build schools and provide educational support in Nepal, the birthplace of Buddha.

<u>Sri Lanka:</u> Provided aid in constructing school buildings damaged by the tsunami. Further, with the help of the Sri Lankan prime minister, 100 bookshelves were donated to Buddhist temples.

<u>India:</u> Ongoing aid since 2006—uniforms, school meals, etc. for schools in Bodh Gaya, a sacred ground for Buddhism. Medical aid in Calcutta, in collaboration with local hospitals.

<u>China:</u> Donated money and tents to the Szechuan Earthquake disaster zone. Books were also donated to elementary schools in Gansu Province, near the disaster zone.

<u>Malaysia:</u> Donated money, educational materials and clothes to local orphanages. Relief supplies were sent to areas in northeast Malaysia, site of the 2015 floods.

<u>Thailand:</u> Constructed libraries and donated books to elementary and junior high schools damaged by floods in Ayutthaya.

<u>Indonesia:</u> Donated to the Sumatra-Andaman Earthquake disaster zone.

**The Philippines:** Donated books and electric fans to elementary schools on Leyte Island in July 2015. Provided aid in the aftermath of Typhoon Haiyan (Yolanda) and donated 5,000 sets of health and hygiene kits.

**Uganda:** Donated educational materials and mosquito nets to protect children from malaria. Offered scholarships to orphans diagnosed with AIDS.

**Kenya:** Donated English copies of Happy Science books, *Invincible Thinking, An Unshakable Mind* and *The Laws of Success* to schools. (Designated as supplementary text by the Kenyan Ministry of Education in July 2014.)

**Ghana:** Provided medical supplies as a preventive measure against Ebola.

**South Africa:** Collaborated with the Nelson Mandela Foundation in South Africa to donate a container library and books to an elementary school.

**Australia:** Donated to the flood-affected northeastern area in 2011 via the Australian Embassy.

**New Zealand:** Donated to the earthquake-stricken area in February 2011 via the New Zealand Embassy.

**Iran:** Donated to the earthquake-stricken area in northeastern Iran in October 2012 via the Iranian Embassy.

**Brazil:** Donated to the flood-affected area in January 2011.

# OTHER ACTIVITIES

Happy Science does other various activities to provide support for those in need.

◆ **You Are An Angel!**
**General Incorporated Association**
Happy Science has a volunteer network in Japan that encourages and supports children with disabilities as well as their parents and guardians.

◆ **Never Mind School for Truancy**
At 'Never Mind,' we support students who find it very challenging to attend schools in Japan. We also nurture their self-help spirit and power to rebound against obstacles in life based on Master Okawa's teachings and faith.

◆ **"Prevention against suicide" campaign since 2003**
A nationwide campaign to reduce suicides; over 20,000 people commit suicide every year in Japan. "The Suicide Prevention Website-Words of Truth for You-" presents spiritual prescriptions for worries such as depression, lost love, extramarital affairs, bullying and work-related problems, thereby saving many lives.

◆ **Support for anti-bullying campaigns**
Happy Science provides support for a group of parents and guardians, Network to Protect Children from Bullying, a general incorporated foundation launched in Japan to end bullying, including those that can even be called a criminal offense. So far, the network received more than 5,000 cases and resolved 90% of them.

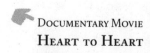

DOCUMENTARY MOVIE
HEART TO HEART

In this documentary movie, Happy Science University students visit these NPO activities to discover what salvation truly is, and on the meaning of life, through heart to heart interviews.

- **The Golden Age Scholarship**
  This scholarship is granted to students who can contribute greatly and bring a hopeful future to the world.

- **Success No.1**
  **Buddha's Truth Afterschool Academy**
  Happy Science has classrooms throughout Japan and in several cities around the world that focus on afterschool education for children. The education focuses on faith and morals in addition to supporting children's school studies.

- **Angel Plan V**
  For children under the age of kindergarten, Happy Science holds classes for nurturing healthy, positive, and creative boys and girls.

- **Future Stars Training Department**
  The Future Stars Training Department was founded within the Happy Science Media Division with the goal of nurturing talented individuals to become successful in the performing arts and entertainment industry.

- **New Star Production Co., Ltd.**
  **ARI Production Co., Ltd.**
  We have companies to nurture actors and actresses, artists, and vocalists. They are also involved in film production.

# MOVIE NEWS

Up to date, Happy Science has produced 18 movies. These projects were all planned by the executive producer, Ryuho Okawa. Our movies have received various awards and recognition around the world.

.....................................

The animation movie, *The Laws of the Universe – Part I*, released simultaneously in Japan and the U.S. in October 2018, has received a total of 5 awards from 4 countries (as of May, 2019). We thank you all for your support, and we wish that this movie can spread even more and people can discover this one and only Truth taught at Happy Science.

**5** Awards from **4** Countries!

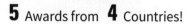

**France**
on
May 18th

NICE INTERNATIONAL FILM FESTIVAL 2019
BEST INTERNATIONAL ANIMATION AWARD

**U.K.**
on
May 25th

LONDON INTERNATIONAL MOTION PICTURE AWARDS 2019
BEST INTERNATIONAL ANIMATION FEATURE FILM AWARD

**India**

CALCUTTA INTERNATIONAL CULT FILM FESTIVAL
[OUTSTANDING ACHIEVEMENT AWARD]

**U.S.**

FILM INVASION LOS ANGELES
[GRAND JURY PRIZE – BEST ANIME FEATURE]

AWARENESS FILM FESTIVAL
[SPECIAL JURY ANIMATION AWARD]

# Lineup of Happy Science Movies

Discover the spiritual world you have never seen and
Come close to the Heart of God through these movies.

•1994•
The Terrifying Revelations
of Nostradamus
(Live-action)

•2016•
I'm Fine, My Angel
(Live-action)

•1997•
Love Blows Like the Wind
(Animation)

•2017•
The World We Live In
(Live-action)

•2000•
The Laws of the Sun
(Animation)

•2018•
Heart to Heart
(Documentary)

•2003•
The Golden Laws
(Animation)

•2018•
DAYBREAK
(Live-action)

•2006•
The Laws of Eternity
(Animation)

•2018•
The Laws of the Universe - Part I
(Animation)

•2009•
The Rebirth of Buddha
(Animation)

•2019•
The Last White Witch
(Live-action)

•2012•
The Final Judgement
(Live-action)

•2019•
Life is Beautiful
- Heart to Heart 2 -
(Documentary)

•2012•
The Mystical Laws
(Animation)

•2019•
Immortal Hero
(Live-action)

•2015•
The Laws of the Universe - Part 0
(Animation)

Contact your nearest local branch for more information on how to watch HS movies.

# CONTACT INFORMATION

Happy Science is a worldwide organization with faith centers around the globe. For a comprehensive list of centers, visit the worldwide directory at *happy-science.org*. The following are some of the many Happy Science locations:

## UNITED STATES AND CANADA

**New York**
79 Franklin St.,
New York, NY 10013
Phone: 212-343-7972
Fax: 212-343-7973
Email: ny@happy-science.org
Website: happyscience-na.org

**San Francisco**
525 Clinton St.,
Redwood City, CA 94062
Phone & Fax: 650-363-2777
Email: sf@happy-science.org
Website: happyscience-na.org

**New Jersey**
725 River Rd, #102B,
Edgewater, NJ 07020
Phone: 201-313-0127
Fax: 201-313-0120
Email: nj@happy-science.org
Website: happyscience-na.org

**Los Angeles**
1590 E. Del Mar Blvd.,
Pasadena, CA 91106
Phone: 626-395-7775
Fax: 626-395-7776
Email: la@happy-science.org
Website: happyscience-na.org

**Florida**
5208 8thSt., Zephyrhills,
FL 33542
Phone: 813-715-0000
Fax: 813-715-0010
Email: florida@happy-science.org
Website: happyscience-na.org

**Orange County**
10231 Slater Ave. #204
Fountain Valley, CA 92708
Phone: 714-745-1140
Email: oc@happy-science.org
Website: happyscience-na.org

**Atlanta**
1874 Piedmont Ave. NE, Suite 360-C
Atlanta, GA 30324
Phone: 404-892-7770
Email: atlanta@happy-science.org
Website: happyscience-na.org

**San Diego**
7841 Balboa Ave., Suite #202
San Diego, CA 92111
Phone: 619-381-7615
Fax: 626-395-7776
E-mail: sandiego@happy-science.org
Website: happyscience-na.org

## Hawaii

Phone: 808-591-9772
Fax: 808-591-9776
Email: hi@happy-science.org
Website: happyscience-na.org

## Kauai

4504 Kukui Street.,
Dragon Building Suite 21,
Kapaa, HI 96746
Phone: 808-822-7007
Fax: 808-822-6007
Email: kauai-hi@happy-science.org
Website: happyscience-na.org

## Toronto

845 The Queensway
Etobicoke, ON M8Z 1N6 Canada
Phone: 1-416-901-3747
Email: toronto@happy-science.org
Website: happy-science.ca

## Vancouver

#212-2609 East 49th Avenue
Vancouver, BC, V5S 1J9, Canada
Phone: 1-604-437-7735
Fax: 1-604-437-7764
Email: vancouver@happy-science.org
Website: happy-science.ca

# INTERNATIONAL

## Tokyo

1-6-7 Togoshi, Shinagawa
Tokyo, 142-0041 Japan
Phone: 81-3-6384-5770
Fax: 81-3-6384-5776
Email: tokyo@happy-science.org
Website: happy-science.org

## London

3 Margaret St.
London,W1W 8RE United Kingdom
Phone: 44-20-7323-9255
Fax: 44-20-7323-9344
Email: eu@happy-science.org
Website: happyscience-uk.org

## Sydney

516 Pacific Hwy, Lane Cove North,
NSW 2066, Australia
Phone: 61-2-9411-2877
Fax: 61-2-9411-2822
Email: sydney@happy-science.org
Website: happyscience.org.au

## South Sao Paulo

Rua. Domingos de Morais 1154,
Vila Mariana, Sao Paulo
SP-CEP 04010-100, Brazil
Phone: 55-11-5574-0054
Fax: 55-11-5088-3806
Email: sp_sul@happy-science.org
Website: happyscience.com.br

**Jundiai**
Rua Congo, 447, Jd. Bonfiglioli
Jundiai-CEP, 13207-340, Brazil
Phone: 55-11-4587-5952
Email: jundiai@happy-science.org

**Uganda**
Plot 877 Rubaga Road, Kampala
P.O. Box 34130, Kampala, Uganda
Phone: 256-79-3238-002
Email: uganda@happy-science.org

**Seoul**
74, Sadang-ro 27-gil,
Dongjak-gu, Seoul, Korea
Phone: 82-2-3478-8777
Fax: 82-2- 3478-9777
Email: korea@happy-science.org

**Thailand**
19 Soi Sukhumvit 60/1,
Bang Chak, Phra Khanong,
Bangkok, 10260 Thailand
Phone: 66-2-007-1419
Email: bangkok@happy-science.org
Website: happyscience-thai.org

**Taipei**
No. 89, Lane 155, Dunhua N. Road.,
Songshan District, Taipei City 105,
Taiwan
Phone: 886-2-2719-9377
Fax: 886-2-2719-5570
Email: taiwan@happy-science.org

**Indonesia**
Darmawangsa
Square Lt. 2 No. 225
Jl. Darmawangsa VI & IX
Indonesia
Phone: 021-7278-0756
Email: indonesia@happy-science.org

**Malaysia**
No 22A, Block 2, Jalil Link Jalan
Jalil Jaya 2, Bukit Jalil 57000, Kuala
Lumpur, Malaysia
Phone: 60-3-8998-7877
Fax: 60-3-8998-7977
Email: malaysia@happy-science.org
Website: happyscience.org.my

**Philippines Taytay**
LGL Bldg, 2nd Floor,
Kadalagaham cor,
Rizal Ave. Taytay,
Rizal, Philippines
Phone: 63-2-5710686
Email: philippines@happy-science.org

**Nepal**
Kathmandu Metropolitan City
Ward No. 15, Ring Road, Kimdol,
Sitapaila Kathmandu, Nepal
Phone: 977-1-427-2931
Email: nepal@happy-science.org

# ABOUT IRH PRESS USA

IRH Press USA Inc. was founded in 2013 as an affiliated firm of IRH Press Co., Ltd. Based in New York, the press publishes books in various categories including spirituality, religion, and self-improvement and publishes books by Ryuho Okawa, the author of over 100 million books sold worldwide. For more information, visit **_okawabooks.com_**.

*Follow us on:*

**Facebook**: Okawa Books          **Twitter**: Okawa Books

**Goodreads**: Ryuho Okawa          **Instagram**: OkawaBooks

**Pinterest**: Okawa Books

## RYUHO OKAWA'S LAWS SERIES

The Laws Series is an annual volume of books that are mainly comprised of Ryuho Okawa's lectures on various topics that highlight principles and guidelines for the activities of Happy Science every year. *The Laws of the Sun*, the first publication of the laws series, ranked in the annual best-selling list in Japan in 1994. Since then, all of the laws series' titles have ranked in the annual best-selling list for more than two decades, setting socio-cultural trends in Japan and around the world.

## THE TRILOGY

The first three volumes of the Laws Series, *The Laws of the Sun*, *The Golden Laws*, and *The Nine Dimensions* make a trilogy that completes the basic framework of the teachings of God's Truths. *The Laws of the Sun* discusses the structure of God's Laws, *The Golden Laws* expounds on the doctrine of time, and *The Nine Dimensions* reveals the nature of space.

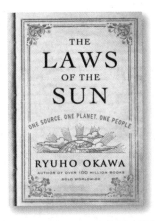

## THE LAWS OF THE SUN

One Source, One Planet, One People

Paperback • 288 pages • $15.95
ISBN: 978-1-942125-43-3

IMAGINE IF YOU COULD ASK GOD why He created this world and what spiritual laws He used to shape us—and everything around us. If we could understand His designs and intentions, we could discover what our goals in life should be and whether our actions move us closer to those goals or farther away.

At a young age, a spiritual calling prompted Ryuho Okawa to outline what he innately understood to be universal truths for all humankind. In *The Laws of the Sun*, Okawa outlines these laws of the universe and provides a road map for living one's life with greater purpose and meaning.

In this powerful book, Ryuho Okawa reveals the transcendent nature of consciousness and the secrets of our multidimensional universe and our place in it. By understanding the different stages of love and following the Buddhist Eightfold Path, he believes we can speed up our eternal process of development. *The Laws of the Sun* shows the way to realize true happiness—a happiness that continues from this world through the other.

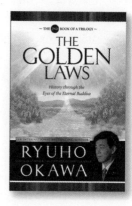

## THE GOLDEN LAWS

History through the Eyes of the Eternal Buddha

Paperback • 216 pages • $14.95
ISBN: 978-1-941779-81-1

Throughout history, Great Guiding Spirits of Light have been present on Earth in both the East and the West at crucial points in human history to further our spiritual development. *The Golden Laws* reveals how Divine Plan has been unfolding on Earth, and outlines 5,000 years of the secret history of humankind. Once we understand the true course of history, through past, present and into the future, we cannot help but become aware of the significance of our spiritual mission in the present age.

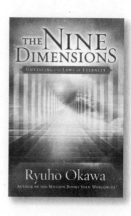

## THE NINE DIMENSIONS

Unveiling the Laws of Eternity

Paperback • 168 pages • $15.95
ISBN: 978-0-982698-56-3

This book is a window into the mind of our loving God, who designed this world and the vast, wondrous world of our afterlife as a school with many levels through which our souls learn and grow. When the religions and cultures of the world discover the truth of their common spiritual origin, they will be inspired to accept their differences, come together under faith in God, and build an era of harmony and peaceful progress on Earth.

## THE CHALLENGE OF THE MIND

An Essential Guide to Buddha's Teachings:
Zen, Karma and Enlightenment

Paperback • 208 pages • $16.95
ISBN: 978-1-942125-45-7

In this book, Ryuho Okawa explains essential Buddhist tenets and how to put these ideas into practice. Enlightenment is not just an abstract idea but one that everyone can experience to some extent. In clear but thought-provoking language, Okawa imbues new life into traditional teachings and offers a solid basis of reason and intellectual understanding to often overcomplicated Buddhist concepts. By applying these basic principles to our lives, we can direct our minds to higher ideals and create a bright future for ourselves and others.

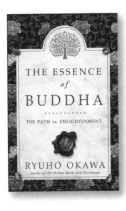

## THE ESSENCE OF BUDDHA

The Path to Enlightenment

Paperback • 208 pages • $14.95
ISBN: 978-1-942125-06-8

In this book, Ryuho Okawa imparts in simple and accessible language his wisdom about the essence of Shakyamuni Buddha's philosophy of life and enlightenment—teachings that have been inspiring people all over the world for over 2,500 years. By offering a new perspective on core Buddhist thoughts that have long been cloaked in mystique, Okawa brings these teachings to life for modern people. *The Essence of Buddha* distills a way of life that anyone can practice to achieve a life of self-growth, compassionate living, and true happiness.

## THE STRONG MIND

The Art of Building the Inner Strength
to Overcome Life's Difficulties

Paperback • 192 pages • $15.95
ISBN: 978-1-942125-36-5

In this book, Ryuho Okawa shares his personal experiences as examples to show how we can build toughness of the heart, develop richness of the mind, and cultivate the power of perseverance. The strong mind is what we need to rise time and again, and to move forward no matter what difficulties we face in life. This book will inspire and empower you to take courage, develop a mature and cultivated heart, and achieve resilience and hardiness so that you can break through the barriers of your limits and keep winning in the battle of your life.

## THE MIRACLE OF MEDITATION

Opening Your Life to Peace, Joy, and
the Power Within

Paperback • 208 pages • $15.95
ISBN: 978-1-942125-09-9

Meditation can open your mind to the self-transformative potential within and connect your soul to the wisdom of heaven—all through the power of belief. This book combines the power of faith and the practice of meditation to help you create inner peace, discover your inner divinity, become your ideal self, and cultivate a purposeful life of altruism and compassion.

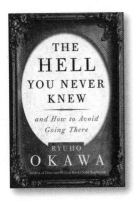

## THE HELL YOU NEVER KNEW

and How to Avoid Going There

Paperback • 192 pages • $15.95
ISBN: 978-1-942125-52-5

From ancient times, people have been warned of the danger of falling to Hell. But does the world of Hell truly exist? If it does, what kind of people would go there? Through his spiritual abilities, Ryuho Okawa found out that Hell is only a small part of the vast Spirit World, yet more than half of the people today go there after they die. Okawa believes the true mission of religion is to save the souls of all people, and eventually, dissolve the world of Hell. That is why he gives the detailed description about the Spirit World, including Heaven and Hell, and encourage people to choose the right path.

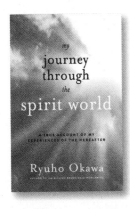

## MY JOURNEY THROUGH THE SPIRIT WORLD

A True Account of
My Experiences of the Hereafter

Paperback • 224 pages • $15.95
ISBN: 978-1-942125-41-9

What happens when we die? What is the afterworld like? Do heaven and hell really exist? In this book, Ryuho Okawa shares surprising facts such as that we visit the spirit world during sleep, that souls in the spirit world go to a school to learn about how to use their spiritual power, and that people continue to live in the same lifestyle as they did in this world. This unique and authentic guide to the spirit world will awaken us to the truth of life and death, and show us how we should start living so that we can return to a bright world of heaven.

## WORRY-FREE LIVING

Let Go of Stress and Live in Peace and Happiness

Hardcover • 192 pages • $16.95
ISBN: 978-1-942125-51-8

We can cultivate peace of mind and attain inner happiness in life, even as we go through life's array of difficult experiences. The wisdom Ryuho Okawa shares in this book about facing problems in human relationships, financial hardships, and other life's stresses will help you change how you look at and approach life's worries and problems for the better. Let this book be your guide to finding precious meaning in all your life's problems, gaining inner growth no matter what you face, and practicing inner happiness and soul-growth all throughout your life.

## MESSAGES FROM HEAVEN

What Jesus, Buddha, Moses, and Muhammad Would Say Today

Hardcover • 224 pages • $19.95
ISBN: 978-1-941779-19-4

If you could speak to Jesus, Buddha, Moses, or Muhammad, what would you ask? In this book, Ryuho Okawa shares the spiritual communication he had with these four spirits and the messages they want to share with people living today. The Truths revealed in this book will open your eyes to a level of spiritual awareness, salvation, and happiness that you have never experienced before.

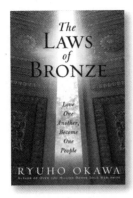

## THE LAWS OF BRONZE

Love One Another, Become One People

Paperback • 224 pages • $15.95
ISBN: 978-1-942125-50-1

With the advancement of science and techno-logy leading to longer life-span, many people are seeking out a way to lead a meaningful life with purpose and direction. This book will show people from all walks of life that they can solve their problems in life both on an individual level and on a global scale by finding faith and practicing love. When all of us in this planet discover our common spiritual origin revealed in this book, we can truly love one another and become one people on Earth.

## LOVE FOR THE FUTURE

Building One World of Freedom and Democracy Under God's Truth

Paperback • 312 pages • $15.95
ISBN: 978-1-942125-60-0

This is a compilation of select international lectures given by Ryuho Okawa during his (ongoing) global missionary tours. While conflicting values of justice exists, this book espouses that freedom and democracy are vital principles for global unification that will resolutely foster peace and shared prosperity, if adopted universally.

# THE LAWS OF INVINCIBLE LEADERSHIP
An Empowering Guide for Continuous and
Lasting Success in Business and in Life


# THE STARTING POINT OF HAPPINESS
An Inspiring Guide to Positive Living with Faith, Love, and Courage


# INVINCIBLE THINKING
An Essential Guide for a Lifetime of Growth, Success, and Triumph


# HEALING FROM WITHIN
Life-Changing Keys to Calm, Spiritual, and Healthy Living


# THE UNHAPPINESS SYNDROME
28 Habits of Unhappy People (and How to Change Them)


# THE LAWS OF SUCCESS
A Spiritual Guide to Turning Your Hopes Into Reality


# THINK BIG!
Be Positive and Be Brave to Achieve Your Dreams


# THE MOMENT OF TRUTH
Become a Living Angel Today


# CHANGE YOUR LIFE, CHANGE THE WORLD
A Spiritual Guide to Living Now


*For a complete list of books, visit **okawabooks.com**.*